# AT YOUR FINGERTIPS

The Catholic Church Rides the Waves of Turbulent History

# AT YOUR FINGERTIPS

## THE CATHOLIC CHURCH RIDES THE
## WAVES OF TURBULENT HISTORY
## (1648-1848)

### VOLUME FOUR

MONSIGNOR LAURENCE J. SPITERI, JCD, PhD

ST PAULS

Library of Congress Cataloging-in-Publication Data

Spiteri, Laurence J.
  At your fingertips: the Catholic Church rides the waves of turbulent history
(1648-1848) / Laurence J. Spiteri.
     p. cm.
  Includes bibliographical references.
  ISBN 978-0-8189-1333-4
1. The Catholic Church rides the waves of turbulent history.  I. Title.
  BR2430.965 2011
  270.6—dc22

                              2010004585

Nihil Obstat:
Michael Downey
Censor Deputatus
December 8, 2010
Imprimatur:
His Eminence
✠ Cardinal Roger M. Mahony
Archbishop of Los Angeles
December 8, 2010

The Nihil Obstat and Imprimatur are official declarations that the work
contains nothing contrary to Faith and Morals. It is not implied thereby
that those granting the Nihil Obstat and Imprimatur agree with the
contents, statements or opinions expressed.

Produced and designed in the United States of America by the
Fathers and Brothers of the Society of St. Paul,
2187 Victory Boulevard, Staten Island, New York 10314-6603
as part of their communications apostolate.

ISBN 10: 0-8189-1333-9
ISBN 13: 978-0-8189-1333-4

**Printing Information:**

| Current Printing - first digit | 1 | 2 | 3 | 4 | 5 | 6 | 7 | 8 | 9 | 1 0 |
|---|---|---|---|---|---|---|---|---|---|---|

Year of Current Printing - first year shown

| 2011 | 2012 | 2013 | 2014 | 2015 | 2016 | 2017 | 2018 | 2019 | 2020 |
|---|---|---|---|---|---|---|---|---|---|

*Knowing history means knowing facts –*
*Understanding history means not to repeat some of them.*

## Dedication

The generation of both my parents
has been called by the Lord to enter eternal life.
These family members gave me, my siblings and our generation
a heritage of a deep faith, a profound commitment to
the Roman Catholic Church, and a treasured heritage
that has touched our personal history.
I dedicate this volume to these wonderful people of faith:
my father Arthur and my mother Mary
and to their siblings – Joseph, Andrew, Ernest,
Mary-Anne, Sisi, Victoria, Emily, Ralph and Romeo
who touched and shaped my life, and to their many siblings
of whom I did not have the privilege to know
because they died before I was born.
Their chapter on the walk in faith, hope and love has been closed.
The chapter of my generation is being written
by the gifted ink of faith, hope and love which the Lord
has bestowed upon each one of us.

# Table of Contents

Preface .................................................................................. ix

Introduction ........................................................................ xv

## SECTION ONE
## POPES PROTECT DOCTRINE AND PROMOTE DEVOTIONS

Chapter 1: The Church and the Enlightenment Clash .............. 3

1. The Catholic Church and the Enlightenment ..................... 4

2. The French Enlightened Philosophers ................................. 6

3. Literature and Literary Activities ...................................... 8

4. Catholic Enlightenment ..................................................11

5. Clash Between the Catholic Church
   and Secular Enlightenment ........................................... 12

Chapter 2: Popes Defend Catholic Doctrine ......................... 17

6. Jansenism .......................................................................17

7. Gallicanism .................................................................. 20

8. Febronianism ............................................................... 22

9. Josephism .................................................................... 24

10. Rome and the Chinese Rites Controversy ....................... 27

Chapter 3: Popes and Our Lady ......................................... 29

11. Mariology.................................................................... 29

12. Roman Catholic Mariology............................................ 34

13. Early Protestant View on Mary ..................................... 36

## SECTION TWO
## POPES DEALING WITH NATIONS

**Chapter 4: Diplomatic Relations** ............................................. **41**

14. Concordats............................................................................ 41

15. Church-State Relations...................................................... 44

16. Selection of Bishops .......................................................... 47

17. The Padroado of Portugal.................................................. 49

18. Concordats during the Eighteenth Century ..................... 51

19. Concordats during the Nineteenth Century...................... 52

**Chapter 5: Rome and Paris**...................................................... **55**

20. Popes and Louis XIV ......................................................... 55

21. Popes and Louis XV ........................................................... 58

22. Pius VI and Revolutionary France ..................................... 61

23. The Occupation of the Papal States .................................. 63

**Chapter 6: Rome and Vienna** .................................................. **67**

24. Popes and Emperor Charles VI .......................................... 67

25. Crisis in Vienna .................................................................. 70

26. Popes and Emperor Joseph II ............................................ 71

**Chapter 7: Rome and Madrid**.................................................. **75**

27. Rome and the Spanish Hapsburgs...................................... 75

28. Latin America Revolts Against Madrid.............................. 78

**Chapter 8: Rome and Lisbon**................................................... **81**

29. Rome Gives into Lisbon's Demands ................................... 81

30. The Portuguese Colonies in Asia....................................... 84

**Chapter 9: Rome and London** ................................................. **87**

31. Catholics Persecuted.......................................................... 87

32. Rome and James II.............................................................. 89

**Chapter 10: Rome and Fragmented Italy** ............................... 93

33. Rome and Italian Principalities ............................................ 93

**Chapter 11: Rome and the United States of America** .............. 99

34. The First American Bishop .............................................. 100

35. American Prejudice ........................................................102

**Chapter 12: The Ottoman Menace** ................................... 105

36. Christianity and the Ottoman Turks ...............................105

**Chapter 13: Napoleon Bonaparte** .....................................111

37. Napoleon ..................................................................... 111

38. Napoleon and Italy .........................................................113

39. First Consul Napoleon .....................................................116

40. Emperor Napoleon I .......................................................118

SECTION THREE
WARS FOR CROWNS

**Chapter 14: European Wars of Succession** ........................... 123

41. The Spanish Crown in Crisis ........................................... 123

42. The War of the Polish Succession .................................... 125

43. The War of the Austrian Succession................................. 127

44. The War of the Bavarian Succession ................................133

SECTION FOUR
POPES AND INTERNAL CHURCH GOVERNANCE

**Chapter 15: Popes Governing the Papal States** ......................141

45. The Dual Role of a Pope ..................................................141

46. Nepotism ..................................................................... 142

47. Cardinals Secretary of State............................................ 144

48. Church Renewal and Reforms .........................................145

49. Ecumenical Efforts........................................................152

**Chapter 16: Meddling in Papal Elections – Veto Powers** ........ 155

50. Electing a Pope ................................................................. 155

51. Veto Powers at Papal Elections .......................................... 158

52. The First Papal Veto ......................................................... 160

53. Continued Secular Interference in Papal Elections ............. 162

**Chapter 17: The Popes and Rome** ........................................... 167

54. The Baroque .................................................................... 167

55. The Rococo ...................................................................... 170

56. Popes as Patrons of the Arts ............................................. 171

57. Jewish Relations .............................................................. 174

SECTION FIVE
THE GLORY OF THE CATHOLIC CHURCH

**Chapter 18: Missionary Activities** .......................................... 179

58. Missions in the Seventeenth Century ................................ 179

59. Missions in the Eighteenth Century .................................. 186

60. Missions in the Americas ................................................. 188

**Chapter 19: Our Shining Stars: Holy Women and Men** ........ 193

61. Saintly People ................................................................. 193

**Appendix: Popes From 1648-1848** ........................................ 205

# Preface

The purpose of the fourth volume in this series echoes that of the previous volumes, namely to provide its reader with a quick and concise reference to some highlights in the history of the Catholic Church with the hope of prompting further and detailed study.[1] The author aims at opening the memory chest of the Church from 1648, the year of the Peace of Westphalia which put universal peace on paper, to the year 1848, when there was already present the heavy and dark clouds of grave instability.

The inner life of the Catholic Church and the international relations of Holy See from the year of peace, 1648, to the year of revolutions, 1848, were like a see-saw. She saw her prestige and influence slip away as the map of Europe and the Americas was redrawn by conquering armies, revolutions, and new masters. She lost many faithful and vast patrimonies as new ideologies rose in their frequent attempts to give her a final mortal blow. Yet, like a seriously wounded soldier, she was brought back to health by her Divine Founder and Healer through courageous lay and religious, members of the hierarchy, inspiring saints, the renewal of spiritual life, and an invisible army of millions of persevering people of faith. These two centuries form a narrative of failure and success, persecution and survival, ungodliness and faith, deceptive piety and authentic devotion, humiliation and victory. It

---

[1]  Though there are many sources in diverse languages which the author consulted in the process of writing this volume, only those in the English language are being identified.

was a period when at times the very foundations of the Catholic Church and society were questioned and threatened but, in the end, the Church continued to grow and prosper even under the most debased conditions.

The Catholic Church of the seventeenth century was faced with some extraordinary events from within that threatened the stability of the Universal Church and, in the case of the Enlightenment and secret societies, the established social order itself. She had to face the heresy of the Enlightenment which questioned Christianity itself. Reason was upheld as the god which was to replace Christianity.[2] Secularism became widespread. The Church also had to confront the perfidious heresy of Jansenism that had taken deep roots in France and in other parts of Europe. Other heresies were also condemned. Moreover, the Church had to face the threat of the increasing attacks on Europe by the Muslim Ottoman Turks. The first secular veto in papal elections was posted in the middle of this century. Yet, despite these threats, the Church was also responding to the faith and needs of her members, using magnificent Baroque techniques to move the hearts, minds, and souls of her faithful toward the contemplation of God's mysteries and the beauty of the Catholic vocation. The reemergence of Marian theology also reinforced private devotions.

During the eighteenth century, various enlightened secular rulers utilized Gallicanism, Febronianism, and Josephism in attempting to encroach on Papal Primacy, and to control the internal life and discipline of the Catholic Church. Gallicanism in France, in comparison to Ultramontanism,[3] advocated

---

2   The Enlightenment movement spread over most of Western Europe, Russia, the North American Colonies, and Latin America.

3   Ultramontanism claimed that the Pope had supreme power even over the secular States.

the restriction of papal supremacy over a nation's Church, if not doing away with it altogether, and endorsed the secular State's authority over religious matters. Febronianism was a version of Gallicanism in the German States. It laid a direct attack on the very identity and role of the Pope and tended toward nationalizing the Catholic Church. Josephism was essentially the application of Febronianism in the Austrian territories by Emperor Joseph II. It aimed at transforming the Catholic Church into an instrument of the secular State. The suppression of the Society of Jesus by Clement XIV in 1773 brought on a devastating negative effect on Catholic education and the Church's missionary activities in Europe and in the missions. The eighteenth century would end by witnessing the brutal French Revolution, the persecution and martyrdom of members of the Roman Catholic hierarchy and laity who remained faithful to Rome, the submission of the Church in France to the Revolutionary government, the Reign of Terror, the rising to power of Napoleon Bonaparte, the beginnings of the reconfiguration of the map of Europe and a new social order, and the imprisonment of Pius VI. These events proved to be the birth pangs of a renewed Church.

The nineteenth century ushered in Napoleon's rise, witnessed his breathtaking conquests and his rapid downfall. It was shaken with wars of successions to major European Crowns, lived through the imprisonment of another Pope, and longed for the restoration of the European pre-French Revolution order, the *Ancien Régime*. The Catholic Church managed to temporarily emerge from the low ebb in her prestige and influence and rampant anticlericalism, and welcomed the restoration of the Society of Jesus. She experienced the re-birth of genuine inner reform and the founding of many religious communities whose members met the desperate and dire needs of a broken European community, and continued her growth in newly emerging nations in the Americas.

As the author's eyes are drawn toward the right hand side of St. Peter's Basilica and beholds the Apostolic Palace, he is reminded that the most important resident within those walls is the direct successor to Peter and the deceased Bishops of Rome. He is the Vicar of Christ to the Universal Church and the person who leads her in unity, charity, and confirmation in her Faith. Some of his predecessors rose successfully to meet the challenges of their contemporary society, while others fell short in this endeavor. Yet, despite human weakness, the Lord Jesus has always triumphed not in the sense of the secular world, but because He is the Lord of all times, all history.

*Mons. Laurence J. Spiteri, JCD, PhD*
Vatican City
21st November 2010
Feast of the Presentation of Mary

# Introduction

It is with great pleasure that I introduce this fourth volume in the series *At Your Fingertips*, a history of the Roman Catholic Church written by Monsignor Laurence J. Spiteri. He is one of my colleagues in my present capacity as Cardinal Librarian and Archivist of the Roman Catholic Church. His current primary responsibility is that of being in charge of the Legal Office of the Vatican Apostolic Library.

When speaking to the youth at Sulmona on 4th July 2010, Pope Benedict XVI told them, "I want to say to you: a Christian is one who has a good memory, who loves history and tries to know it."[1] These words are so true! We feel saddened when persons lose their memory. They cannot recognize anyone and cannot recall happy, as well as sad, occasions and celebrations. Everything is always new to them and so, there remains a real risk that the same mistakes be repeated over and over again. Since they lack insight because they cannot recall the past, they also lack understanding. How distressing and tragic! This is all the more terrible when a nation lacks memory because it loses its ability to claim its own particular history. On the other hand, when an individual or a nation attempts to reconstruct its history, to suppress certain events or invent new ones, such acts render an orphan the history

---

[1] Libreria Editrice Vaticana, "*Meeting with the Young People – Address of His Holiness Benedict XVI*," Cathedral of Sulmona, 4th July 2010.

of today. They cause today's history as not being the inheritor of yesterdays and yester-years. The emergence and development of personal or national identity is made a blank.

Monsignor Spiteri identifies the purpose of this fourth volume entitled, *The Catholic Church Rides the Waves of Turbulent History*, as being the unlocking of the memory chest of the Church from 1648 to 1848. As he has done so refreshingly well in his previous three volumes, he does so again with clarity, insight, conciseness, and respect for historical facts. This volume, like the previous ones, is delightful to read and most informative.

During these two hundred years, Catholic princes and other secular authorities rebelled against Rome, but did not go into formal schism. Some unsuccessfully tried to control her. The Church of this historic era, like the Church of today, was faced with oppression, tension, and severe problems from without and within. The Church was quickly losing its moral and political authority. Politicians and those seeking self-promotion and acquisition of power looked at the moral force of the Church as an obstacle that had to be removed or neutralized or at least discounted. It seemed that the winds which blew forward the barge of Peter were not only to be stilled but that the barge itself would capsize and sink. Yet, despite the very low nadir to which the Papacy and the Catholic Church had fallen, there were strong indications of great expectations and undertakings. Wonderful achievements were being materialized despite great adversity, inner Church controversies, and most discomforting situations. Divine Providence sent great saintly men and women, churchmen, preachers, missionaries, scholars, and artists that not only added a silver lining to the dark cloud that hung over the Church but also dispelled some of the darkness that hovered over her.

The memory chest of the Church of this particular historic period does not only contain pain and sorrow but also hope and promise because, in the end, it is the finger of God who guides and protects her. Let us then, as Pope Benedict XVI stated, have a good memory, love history, and understand it. This volume helps us to do so.

*Cardinal Raffaele Farina, SDB*
Cardinal Librarian and Archivist
of the Roman Catholic Church
Vatican City
16th December 2010

SECTION ONE

# Popes Protect Doctrine and Promote Devotions

# CHAPTER ONE

# The Church and the Enlightenment Clash

The Enlightenment[1] is a term coined in the middle of the nineteenth century. It refers to a period in Western civilization that witnessed the presence of a number of divergent philosophies and a cultural way of life emerging from the Scientific Revolution. It offered a value system, rather than a set of ideas, through an assortment of philosophies which, on many occasions, seemed to contradict one another. At its core was a critical questioning of traditional institutions, customs, and morals. Reason, along with science and humanity, were viewed as being supreme over any established authority, spiritual and secular. Reason, however, was viewed as the supreme source for authority. Some historians have referred to it as the last major heresy in Europe, lacking objective and enduring truths. Members of the Enlightenment were convinced that they were emerging from centuries of darkness and ignorance.

---

[1] See Cross, F.L. and E.A. Livingstone (eds.), *The Oxford Dictionary of the Christian Church*, (henceforth *ODCC*) 2nd ed., OUP (1978), "Enlightenment"; H. Lindsell, *The New Paganism*, SF: Harper & Row (1987); P. Gay, *The Enlightenment: The Rise of Modern Paganism*, Alfred A. Knopf, Inc. (1995); I. Rivers, *Reason, Grace, and Sentiment: A Study of the Language of Religion and Ethics*, CPU (2000); R. Potter, *The Creation of the Modern World*, Norton (2000); idem., *The Enlightenment*, Palgave Macmillan (2001); J. Melton, *The Rise of the Public in Enlightenment Europe*, CUP (2001); P. Levillain (ed.), "Innocent X," in *The Papacy: An Encyclopedia*, Routledge (2002); *The Columbia Encyclopedia*, 6th ed. CUP (2004) (henceforth *CE*), "Enlightenment"; D. Beales, E. Derek, *Enlightenment and Reform in 18th Century Europe*, I.B. Tauris (2005).

The movement began around the middle of the seventeenth century and lasted roughly until the beginning of the Napoleonic Wars in 1804. The original proponents usually gathered in salons where women organized discussion groups. Objective truths, particularly divinely revealed truths, had no standing. The movement developed more or less simultaneously in England, Germany, France, Spain, the Netherlands, Italy, and Portugal. It eventually reached Russia, the Polish-Lithuanian Commonwealth, Scandinavia, and Latin America. Some historians propose that the principles of the Enlightenment motivated the signatories of the American Declaration of Independence, the United States Bill of Rights, the French Declaration of the Rights of Man and of the Citizen, and the 1791 Polish-Lithuanian Constitution.

The early Enlightenment was deeply rooted in the Scientific Revolution, and influenced in the beginning by Britain, especially by John Locke's *Essay Concerning Human Understanding*. The work claimed that an individual is a blank slate at birth (*tabula rasa*) and thus, is shaped by education. Eventually, people like Voltaire[2] and Jean-Jacques Rousseau picked up this notion.

## 1. The Catholic Church and the Enlightenment

The Enlightenment presented a new challenge to the Catholic Church. While the Protestant Reformation questioned a number of Catholic doctrines and ancient customs, the Enlightenment doubted Christianity itself. Everything was open to a critical examination by the public in rapidly changing societies due to the Industrial Revolution. Ironically, these philosophers thought that

---

[2]  Francois-Marie Arouet was known as Voltaire.

they had a better grasp than the public at large of what constitutes the public sphere, thereby replacing religious dogmas with a set of their own. The Enlightenment elevated human reason above Divine Revelation and downgraded religious authorities such as the Papacy. It argued that religious doctrine had circumscribed thinking and that henceforth reason and rationality should be applied to every problem seeking resolution. At this time, the Papacy also had to confront Gallicanism and Conciliarism[3] which threatened the role of the Papacy and the structure of the Catholic Church. But the threats reached beyond the Church. Enlightenment ideals, which could be summarized in the writings of "the Republic of Letters," aimed at establishing an egalitarian realm governed by knowledge that could act across political boundaries and rival state powers. Secular rulers were forced to be on guard. Writers who participated in the Republic of Letters, such as Denis Diderot and Voltaire, formed a microcosm of the larger "republic."

The French Revolution, propelled by Enlightenment ideals, was outright against anything related to the established order, harboring a singular hate of the Catholic Church. Its anti-clericalism led to the blanket confiscation of Catholic Church property and attempted to establish a French state-run Church. When large numbers of Catholic clergy refused to take an oath of compliance to the National Assembly, France declared the Church outlawed, replaced it with a new religion that worshipped Reason, destroyed numerous monasteries and convents, forced thousands of Catholic

---

[3]  See J. Brotton, *The Renaissance: A Very Short Introduction*, London: OUP (2006); *ODCC*, "Conciliarism"; L.J. Spiteri, *At Your Fingertips: A History of the Roman Catholic Church until the Council of Trent* (henceforth, *At Your Fingertips* I), NY: ST PAULS/Alba House (2008), nn. 62, 63; idem., *At Your Fingertips: The Triumphs and Intrigues of the Renaissance Popes* (henceforth, *At Your Fingertips* II), NY: ST PAULS/Alba House (2010), nn. 4-9, 60, 62, 63.

clerics into exile, and executed hundreds who had been hunted
down like animals.

When Pius VI condemned the French Revolution and what
it stood for, Napoleon Bonaparte[4] invaded the Papal States. The
Pope became a French prisoner in February 1799. Pius VI died
a virtual prisoner in Valence. Yet, no matter how the French
Revolution and Napoleon treated the Catholic French Church,
it was there to stay. The end of Napoleon's power, signaled with
the beginning of Congress of Vienna in September 1814, brought
a Catholic revival, renewed enthusiasm, and new respect for the
papacy.

---

## 2. The French Enlightened Philosophers

The enlightened European sovereigns were despots who vigorously
tried to impose their program, many a time in a high-handed
style. France, perhaps, produced the more renowned enlightened
philosophers.

An early leader of the French Enlightenment was Baron
Charles Louis de Montesquieu. Though a nobleman, he was inspired by the British political system, advocated a constitutional
French monarchy but, in disagreement with the British policy,
was anti-slavery. Another Enlightenment leader, Voltaire, died a
decade before the outbreak of the French Revolution. Though
educated by the Jesuits, he hated the Catholic Church with a
passion and encouraged its destruction while, ironically, advocating religious toleration. He was antagonized by the revolutionary

---

[4]  See nn. 38-39.

and deeply emotionally troubled Rousseau. Strongly advocating the abolition of the French monarchy and the establishment of a direct democracy, Rousseau's ideas helped shape the most radical elements of the French Revolution. He, like Voltaire, died before the outbreak of the Revolution that toppled the French monarchy and began an ardent persecution of the Catholic Church.

Perhaps one of the best known achievements of the secular French Enlightenment was the *Encyclopedia*, with Diderot as its editor. The first edition, published in 1751, had people like Voltaire, Montesquieu, and Rousseau as contributors. The principal purpose of the publication was to spread the Enlightenment beyond the boundaries of France. Copies found their way as far as Russia and the American English Colonies. However, the work was roundly censured throughout Europe due to some of its radical contents.

Many countries produced prominent persons during the Enlightenment. France had the mathematician and physicist Jean le Rond d'Alembert, one of the editors of the *Encyclopedia*; Pierre Bayle, who advocated religious tolerance; and the politician, philosopher, and mathematician Marquis de Condorcet. Great Britain produced the writer and diarist James Boswell; the politician and philosopher Edmund Burke; the historian Edward Gibbon; the philosopher Thomas Hobbes; the philosopher, historian, and economist David Hume; the philosopher John Locke; and the writer, philosopher, political activist and feminist Mary Wollstonecraft. Germany had the ecclesiastical jurist Justus Henning Boehmer, one of the first reformers of Church and civil law; and the philosopher and physicist Immanuel Kant. Spain produced the botanic explorer José Celestino Mutis; the statesman Gaspar Melchor de Jovellanos; and the writer Leandro Fernández de Moratín. Poland provided the educator Hugo Kołłątaj; and the poet Ignacy Krasicki. The United States had the statesman, scientist, author, and revolutionary leader Benjamin Franklin; the statesman and philosopher James Madison; and the statesman Thomas Jefferson. There were also, among many others, the Portuguese Sebastião de Melo, Marquis of Pombal; the Dutch philosopher Balthasar Bekker; the Russian philanthropist Nikolay Novikov; the Romanian Dimitrie Cantemir; the Swedish botanist and zoologist Carl Linnaeus; and the Serbian philosopher and linguist Dositej Obradović. This short list provides a flavor of how widespread the secular Enlightenment movement became.

Women, especially in France, played a key role in the establishment of the Enlightenment, by not only providing places for meetings but also assisting in avoiding censorship. Their role, however, was barely acknowledged! Rousseau stated that they should not be granted equal education to that of men.

## 3. Literature and Literary Activities

(a) The establishment of the Academy of Science in Paris in 1666 initiated the history of Academies in France during the Enlightenment. The rise of the French Academies went hand-in-hand with the rising interest in science and an increasing secularization. But, the Academies were open only to elite scholars and identified themselves as the best equipped to interpret the sciences for the people. The *Academie francaise* revived a practice that dated back to the Middle Ages when it sought public contests. These contests were on the subjects of religion and monarchy. They expanded to include such topics as poetry, royal propaganda, philosophical issues, essays on social and political issues, and paintings by the middle of the eighteenth century. They avoided controversial topics like slave trade, women's education, and French justice. The contests were open to everyone. Material was submitted anonymously to elite judges for a fair evaluation. A number of women managed to win some competitions.

The British Royal Society of London played a crucial role in the public sphere and helped to disseminate Enlightenment ideas. It promoted Robert Boyle's experimental philosophy all over Europe, and acted as a conduit for intellectual correspondence and exchange. Boyle based knowledge on empirical experiments, a method which remains the basis for our own modern-day scientists. But, as in the case with France, his approach was very elitist.

One major reason for the rapid spreading of Enlightenment ideas was the Industrial Revolution that provided low-cost production of books, pamphlets, newspapers, and journals which contained ideas about many topics. The demand for such material increased as more people moved to the city, where they assumed gainful, though much oppressive, work. Reading became extensive and public libraries increased and became somewhat popular. These libraries began to loan their material for a small fee. But, there was always the threat of State censorship, especially in despotic France. Publishers and sellers had to come up with ingenious clandestine methods for printing and selling critical literature on the establishment at home and beyond national borders. The *Encyclopedia* was paradoxically saved from censorship by the very man in charge of it, Chrétien-Guillaume de Lamoignon de Malesherbes!

(b) The first English coffeehouse, named Angel, was established in Oxford in 1650. Scholars discussed Enlightenment ideas in an informal setting. Coffee reached France in the 1640s. The first French café house, Café Procope, was established in 1686, becoming a center of the Enlightenment. Diderot and d'Alembert decided to create the *Encyclopedia* while visiting the Café.[5] People like Jean-Paul Marat, Jacques-René Hébert, and Camille Desmoulins frequented the place during the Revolution. Cafés also served as places for recruiting young naive intellectuals to revolutionary ideals and their cause. There were also other groups open to the common people, providing them with an opportunity to share their opinions on how societies should be constituted. Such groups, like the Debating societies which appeared in London in 1780, became very popular.

(c) Scientific literature arose in importance as the Enlightenment ideas began to spread. Natural History appealed to the French upper classes, but it also geared itself to make political comments, slipping from the natural world to the social order, and advocating the superiority of the natural over the social state of affairs. Natural scientists took the opportunity to develop and propose their own social ideals which were based on their scientific work.

Scientific and literary periodicals and journals began to exert a great sway on the European intellectual culture, starting around 1680. French and Latin were the main languages of publication, with French dominating the field in due course. Periodicals in German and Dutch were also in steady demand. England kept to itself. The major impact the publications had on European society shaped the way literate people began looking at life. The movement advocated replacing authority with public opinion, the superiority of scientific ideals and toleration, the criticism

---

[5] Some of the more famous encyclopaedists were Blondel, Diderot, Guillaume le Blond, Rousseau, Baron d'Holbach, Montesquieu, Jean-Baptiste de la Chapelle, Toussaint, Anne Robert Jacques Turgot (Laune), and Voltaire.

of universal truths as being manipulated by the State and the Churches, and that the new knowledge bestowed through science and reason was superior to any kind of existing authority. This was a real threat not only to Churches, in particular to the Catholic Church, but also to secular governments.

---

## 4. Catholic Enlightenment

The Catholic Enlightenment was a heterogeneous phenomenon during the *Ancien Régime* in Europe and Latin America[6] when an enlightened Catholic monarch and/or his ministers, along with some Roman Catholic clergy, pushed to find answers to the rapid spreading of secularism and to counteract the rationalism being promoted by the secular Enlightenment. The members of the Catholic Enlightenment aimed at reconciling what they perceived as conflicting concepts of reason and Divine Revelation. Unfortunately, the program pushed for nationalized Catholic Churches and attacked Papal Primacy. They claimed justification for these ideas because secular Enlightenment challenged the very foundations of Christianity and specifically the Catholic Church.

Secular Enlightenment was generally not anti-God, but it was certainly anti-Christian, especially anti-Catholic. It claimed that many tenets of the Catholic Church were fictitious because they were merely man-made. Many of the most influential philosophers of that time were secularists. Many of them promoted a deist view, affirming that the only revelation of God was na-

---

6 The *Ancien Régime* was essentially the political and social system that existed in Europe before the French Revolution of 1789. The term is usually associated with the political and social system in France at the time.

ture and that the Catholic Church's claim to Divine Revelation was fictitious. They claimed that the Catholic Church, and in particular the Jesuits, obstructed the advance of science, the freedom of thought, and the arts. Ironically, the Jesuits of the time were known for their academic triumphs. Protestant churches in Northern Europe saw fit to join forces with the strong critics of the Catholic Church and thereby deflected any criticism of their churches.

## 5. Clash Between the Catholic Church and Secular Enlightenment

The Catholic Church by definition is world-wide. She stood in contract to the contemporary Protestant churches that were disjointed, austere, provincial and plain in their respective thinking and identity. The Catholic Church of the time was splendid in its baroque tastes and colorful in the celebration of its many feasts and religious processions. The Enlightenment, negating the divine origins of the Catholic Church, saw her religious expressions as being based on the human senses and, therefore, illusionary and deceiving. The Church became at risk of being replaced by the notions of the liberal intelligentsia. Many within the Church came to its defense, but the Jesuits occupied first place. They upheld Papal Primacy and led the Ultramontane movement. Since their founding in the mid-sixteenth century, Jesuits rose to occupy key roles in the administrative machinery of secular States, in higher education institutions, and in the Church in every Catholic nation. They were often the most influential confessors at Catholic royal courts. They were answerable only to the Roman Pontiff. But they also had gained a reputation of being elitist, secretive, unscrupulous, and obsessed with power. Perceived as staunchly obstructionist of anything that endangered the Papacy and the Catholic Faith, they became the target of intrigue and intense hate of their enemies within the Church, at many Catholic royal courts, and of the secular Enlightenment. These groups were determined to destroy the Jesuits' influence and to suppress the Society of Jesus. The attack within the Catholic world was led by four statesmen and Emperor Joseph II.

(a) The prime minister of Portugal, Marques de Pombal, expelled the Jesuits from Portugal and its colonial empire and confiscated their assets in 1759.[7] When he failed to persuade the Pope to suppress the Society of Jesus, and despite the binding concordat between the Holy See and Portugal, he broke off diplomatic relations with Rome until 1770. In the meantime he reorganized the educational system in Portugal and its colonies.

(b) The Austrian chancellor Count Wenzel Anton von Kaunitz worked hand-in-hand with Emperor Joseph II to establish Josephism.[8] They considered themselves enlightened. Their most unpopular project was the attempt to reform the Catholic Church in Austria and make the Church independent of Rome and a tool of the State. While the emperor considered himself the guardian of the Catholic Church, he tried his best to usurp papal prerogatives. Pius VI traveled to that country in 1782 to hold talks with the emperor and his chancellor. Joseph II refused to be swayed by the Pope's pleas. Furthermore, he showed himself very friendly

---

[7] See H.V. Livermore, *A New History of Portugal*, CUP (1969); K. Maxwell, *Pombal, Paradox of the Enlightenment*, CUP (1995); Breton, A. (ed.), *Nationalism and Rationality*, CUP (1995); Beales, Derek, *op. cit.*

[8] See R. Kann, *A History of the Hapsburg Empire, 1526-1918*, UCLA (1974); B. Dawson, E. Derek, *Joseph II: In the Shadow of Maria Theresa, 1741-1780*, CUP (1987); Beales, Derek, *op. cit.*; J. Berenger, *A History of the Hapsburg Empire, 1700-1918* (C. Simpson, trans.), NY: Longmans (1997); C.W. Ingrao, *The Hapsburg Monarchy, 1618-1815*, NY: CUP (2000); R. Okey, *The Hapsburg Monarchy c. 1765-1918*, NY: Palgrave MacMillan (2002).

toward the anti-Catholic Freemasonry because he found it to be highly compatible with his personal agenda.

(c) The chief minister of Louis XV, Duke Etienne-Francois de Choiseul, was a known hater of the Jesuits and a great proponent of the French members of the Enlightenment.[9] Though his foreign policy was disastrous for France, his home policy satisfied the French anti-Catholic philosophers. He got the Jesuits banned from France and was one of those who persuaded Clement XIV to suppress their Society. His fall from power was due to his anti-Jesuit policies, and to his support of the Jansenist Louis-René La Chalotais and the provincial parliaments. After the death of the anti-Jesuit Madame de Pompadour[10] in 1764, his enemies, led by Madame du Barry[11] and the chancellor René Maupeou, proved to be too strong for him. Consequently, he lost his powerful office.

(d) The fourth statesman to attack the Catholic Church was Bernardo Tanucci.[12] He served for many years as prime minister of the Kingdom of the Two Sicilies. He did everything within his power to curtail and reduce the power of the Church within the kingdom and to have the Jesuits suppressed in all the Bourbon territories, which included France, Spain, Parma, and all their colonies. Tanucci was resolute to govern the kingdom on the principles of enlightened absolutism, to establish the State's supremacy over the Church, to abolish papal feudal privileges, to

---

[9] See O. Bernier, *Louis the Beloved: The Life of Louis XV*, NY: Doubleday (1984); C. Jones, *The Great Nation: France from Louis XV to Napoleon*, Penguin (2001); Beales, Derek, op. cit.

[10] See C.P. Algrant, *Madame de Pompadour: Mistress of France*, Grove Press (2002).

[11] See J. Haslip, *Madame du Barry: The Wages of Beauty*, NY: Grove Weidenfeld (1992); Bernier, op. cit.

[12] See J. Lynch, *Bourbon Spain, 1700-1808*, Oxford: Basil Blackwell (1989); *Encyclopaedia Britannica*, (2010) "Bernardo, Marquess Tanucci."

restrict the jurisdiction of bishops, to suppress male and female contemplative communities, and to do away with all taxation forwarded to Rome. The kingdom signed a concordat with the Holy See in 1741, but Tanucci went beyond the concordat. Papal documents required the crown's prior approval before publishing them in the kingdom, Naples ceased to be a papal fiefdom, appeals to Rome required the Crown's prior permission, revenues from vacant bishoprics and abbeys went to the Crown, contemplative communities were suppressed, Church tithes were abolished and she could no longer inherit new lands by mortmain, and marriage was declared a civil contract and independent of Church law. His autocratic policy met much success. He convinced Ferdinand IV to have as his first act upon reaching majority[13] the expulsion of the Jesuits in 1767.

Tanucci occupied the papal territories of Benevento and Pontecorvo in response to being excommunicated by Clement XIII.[14] On the other hand, the bishops in the kingdom protested against the new teachings introduced in the Neapolitan schools. Tanucci simply dismissed their protests. One of his final acts before his fall from power in 1776 was to abolish the yearly tribute that the Crown had given to Rome since the time of Charles of Anjou in the thirteenth century.

---

[13] Ferdinand became king at age eight in 1759 when his father forfeited his throne in order to become King Charles III of Spain.

[14] These territories were not returned to the Catholic Church until Clement XIV suppressed the Society of Jesus in 1773.

# CHAPTER TWO

# Popes Defend Catholic Doctrine

## 6. Jansenism

The revival of Catholic life as envisioned by the Counter-Reformation in France began soon after the dawn of the seventeenth century. It sprouted at the grass-roots level. Once the revival got started, its wonderful ramifications were vast. They affected the lives of the common people, the nobility, the religious, and the hierarchy. New forms of religious life and of preparing candidates for the priesthood soon emerged. One notable innovation, which began around 1620 and came to an end around 1665, was the *Compagnie du Saint-Sacrement*, led by the laity. Over three hundred years later, similar lay directed movements arose again, where clergy became members of such communities.[1] The Company developed in part from frustration with the apparent slow pace of Tridentine reform measures of the period. The Company became well known for its corporal works of mercy, the support of home and overseas missions, and moral reform.

France would give the Catholic Church a long list of saints, religious founders, and inner Church reform despite the fact that

---

[1] For example, the Focolare Movement, the Comunione e Liberazione Movement, and the Neocatechumenate Movement of the later twentieth century.

the Church would face great trials and crises during this same time frame. The first big stumbling block to the Catholic religious revival in France was Jansenism.[2]

Michael Baius was a Belgian theologian whose unorthodox writings, particularly on grace and free will, formed the background for Jansenism which arose many years after his death. Baius, a 1552 imperial appointee for Scripture at the University of Leuven, attempted to reinterpret the teachings of St. Augustine. He was appointed as one of the Belgian representatives for the third and final phase of the Council of Trent in 1563. Though he arrived too late to contribute anything of substance, the Council Fathers perceived him as being unorthodox. St. Pius V condemned seventy-nine of his propositions. Baius later submitted, but due to some subsequent comments made by him and his supporters, Gregory XIII condemned them a second time in 1579. When evaluated from a Catholic perspective, the writings were a mix of Catholic orthodoxy with a good dosage of Protestant leanings. His teaching, with its full implications, appeared in Bishop Jansen's posthumously published heretical book, *Augustinus*, in 1640.

Innocent X condemned five Jansenist propositions with the Papal Bull *Cum Occasione* in May 1653.[3] This was the beginning of a process, sought by Louis XIV of France and many French churchmen, that ended with the razing of the Jansenist convent of Port-Royal and the disbanding of its community. The greatest opponents of Jansenism were the Jesuits who, in fact, coined

---

[2]  See J. Hardman, *French Politics: 1774-1789*, Longman (1995); J. McManners, *Church and Society in 18th Century France*, Vol. I, OUP (1999); W. Doyle, *Jansenism*, London: Macmillan (2000); *At Your Fingertips: The Catholic Counter-Reformation* (henceforth: *At Your Fingertips* III), NY: ST PAULS/Alba House (2010), n. 46; *ODCC*, "Jansenism."

[3]  See P. Levillain (ed.), "Innocent X"; op. cit.; *ODCC*, "Innocent X," "Jansenism."

the term for this heresy which managed to spread rapidly on continental Europe.

Two of the condemned five propositions were in Jansen's *Augustinus*, while the other three were inherently present. In essence, the heresy stated the impossibility for man to obey God's commandments without a Divine special grace, and that the operation of grace is irresistible because man is the victim of a natural or a supernatural limited determinism which is not violently coercive. The heresy was pessimistic, harsh, and morally rigorist in nature. For an adherer, the resistance to receive Holy Communion was more meritorious than receiving the Eucharist, a confession without perfect contrition was useless, and absolution was to be withheld until the penance was completed. The Jesuits raised the alarm against the heresy. Jansenists perceived them as their mortal enemy and became determined to bring about their suppression.

The first generation of French Jansenists was led by Saint-Cyran. Antoine Arnauld succeeded him in 1643. The Sorbonne issued the first condemnation of Jansenism in 1649. Innocent X officially condemned the heresy in 1653. The Jansenists then began dogging this decision by utilizing mental reservations and deceit. Jansenists agreed that the five propositions were heretical in nature but claimed that these did not embody Jansen's teachings. The Jesuits kept attacking the underlying issues of the heresy and its adherers. Thus, Alexander VII issued another condemnation in 1656 and sent an anti-Jansenist formula to be sworn and signed by all French clergy. There was public opposition to the formula and Blaise Pascal wrote in defense of Jansenism. Further papal condemnations followed. Though Jansenists were swayed into a qualified submission to authentic Catholic doctrine in 1668, they gained more sympathizers among the French Catholic hierarchy.

Pasquier Quesnel reaffirmed all the substantive teachings of Jansenism in 1693. Clement XI[4] issued another condemnation in 1713 by his Bull, *Unigenitus*. When the Jansenists refused to accept the decree, Louis XIV increased their persecution by secular authorities, which continued for most of the eighteenth century. However, many fled and joined their counterparts in the Netherlands where they eventually established their heretical church in 1723. But their greatest success was in Tuscany which at the time was ruled by Grand Duke Leopold of Austria.

Other contemporary doctrines were also condemned. Blessed Innocent XI,[5] in 1679, publicly condemned sixty-five Casuist propositions, taken chiefly from the writings of Antonio Escobar y Mendoza and Thomas Sanchez who basically promoted a convenient lax morality that might justify any kind of behavior in a given case. There was the papal condemnation in 1687 of sixty-eight Quietist propositions of Miguel de Molinos[6] who taught intellectual stillness and interior passivity as essential conditions of spiritual perfection, thereby practically eliminating human cooperation with God's grace.

### 7. Gallicanism

Gallicanism has a very long history in France, dating back to privileges that Popes had granted to the Frankish Kings and some bishops.[7] The papal privileges became known as the Gallican

---

4   See J.N.D. Kelly, *The Oxford Dictionary of Popes*, OUP (1993), "Innocent XI"; P. Levillain (ed.), "Clement XI."
5   P. Levillain (ed.), "Innocent XI."
6   See *ODCC*, "Quietism"; Kelly, op. cit., "Innocent XI."
7   See *ODCC*, "Gallicanism"; N.M. Sutherland, *Princes, Politics and Religion, 1547-*

Liberties, which are the basis for Gallicanism. As time passed, succeeding Popes began slowly restricting these privileges. Some French rulers realized that this policy restricted the powers of the French Crown. Thus, French bishops became persuaded over time by their sovereign to support the Gallican movement. The former failed to see that independence of Rome meant servitude to the French Crown. The Gallican principles took a definite form in the time of the Great Western Schism. They were reinforced by the Conciliarist Movement. Despite many papal efforts to procure the withdrawal of excessive demands, most of the Gallican Liberties remained in force till the 1516 Concordat of Bologna. The long delay of the promulgation of the Tridentine Decrees in France was partly due to the prevalent Gallican mentality in the country.

Gallicanism was renewed in the beginning of the seventeenth century when Cardinal Richelieu's domestic policy kept it alive among the French clergy. The long reign of Louis XIV marked a new impetus in the history of the Gallican Liberties. France snatched more and more power from the Holy See. Blessed Innocent XI continuously and futilely insisted on Papal Primacy while the absolute Louis XIV extended his regal authority and carried out his Gallican policies at whim. The French clergy adopted the four articles known as the Gallican Liberties of 1682 which, in effect, annulled Papal Primacy. The Pope declared them null and void.[8]

---

*1589,* London: Hambledon Press (1984); J.J. Hughes, *Pontiffs: Popes Who Shaped History,* Huntington: OSV (1994); J.R. Major, *From Renaissance Monarchy to Absolute Monarchy: French Kings, Nobles and Estates,* Baltimore: JHU Press (1997); R. Po-chia Hsia, *The World of Catholic Renewal, 1540-1770,* Cambridge (1998); J.H. Sheenan, *The Bourbons: The History of a Dynasty,* Continuum (2008); *CE,* "Gallicanism"; Spiteri, *At Your Fingertips* I, n. 54; idem., *At Your Fingertips* III, n. 47.

[8]  See n. 20 (c).

## 8. Febronianism

What started in France as a spirit of opposition to the Holy See in the form of Gallicanism and Jansenism soon spread to various principalities of the Holy Roman Empire.[9] The Reformation and the imminent danger of heresy had united the Catholics of Germany to cling more closely to Rome. But once the Peace of Westphalia took effect,[10] German Catholic rulers, including the Prince-Bishops, began taking measures to secure more of their personal powers, independent of papal authority, rather than safeguard the interests of the Church in their respective domains. They got their inspiration from their Protestant counterparts who were supreme rulers in both temporal and spiritual matters.

John Nicholas von Hontheim had been a student of Zeger Bernhard van Espen, the famed Gallican and Jansenist professor at the University of Leuven. He was entrusted with various important offices by the Prince-Bishop of Trier, before becoming his auxiliary bishop in 1740. At the time there was some hope for unification between German Lutherans and Catholics. Von Hontheim took on this task. He weakened Papal authority because it was perceived as a major obstacle to a reunion and instead promoted Gallicanism to make the unification acceptable to moderate believers of both Creeds. He published his book entitled *De statu ecclesiae et de legitima potestate Romani Pontificis*, under the pen name of Justinus Febronius, in 1762.

---

[9] See H. Holborn, *A History of Modern Germany: 1648-1840*, PUP (1982); D.E.D. Beales, *Enlightenment and Reform in 18th Century Europe*, NY: I.B. Tauris & Co. Ltd. (2005); D.E.D. Beales and G. Best, *History, Society, and the Churches*, CUP (2005); *ODCC*, "Febronianism"; *CE*, "Febronianism."

[10] See D. Croxton, *Peacemaking in Early Modern Europe: Cardinal Mazarin and the Congress of Westphalia, 1643-1648*, Selinsgrove: Susquehanna University Press (1999); Spiteri, *At Your Fingertips* III, n. 58.

Febronius taught that Christ entrusted the power of the keys to the entire Church which in turn handed over its administration to the Pope and his bishops; that all bishops were equal and governed their dioceses independently, with the Pope, as first among equals, occupying a primacy of honor for the sake of unity; that the primacy of honor could be transferred from Rome to any other diocese; that the Pope did not enjoy universal jurisdiction for the latter was based on forged documents; that the Pope was subject to General Councils; and that should he refuse to give up his false claims, bishops could seek assistance from civil authorities to force the Pope to give them up. In essence, Febronius was resorting to the imposition of Conciliarism. Since the book advocated that the Catholic Church was subservient to the secular State, it was received with great acclaim by many secular rulers and their collaborators.

Clement XIII[11] condemned the teachings of Febronius in 1764 and urged the Catholic German bishops to take strong measures to stamp out the erroneous doctrine. Though some bishops were either in favor of Febronius or indifferent, most of them condemned it in their own dioceses. Several authors also published writings rejecting Febronianism. Yet Febronius' work was published again and translated into German, Italian, French, Spanish, and Portuguese. Though the Pope succeeded to convince the Prince-Bishop of Trier to make von Hontheim retract his teachings in 1778, many of his followers claimed that the retraction was null by reason of undue pressure. The bishop published a commentary wherein he explained the reasons for his retraction and ended up re-affirming his original position.

---

[11] P. Levillain (ed.), "Clement XIII"; *ODCC*, "Clement XIII"; *CE*, "Clement XIII."

Nonetheless, before he died in 1790, he did express his sincere regret for his teachings and died in full communion with the Catholic Church.

## 9. Josephism

Often, during the reigns of Emperors Leopold I, Joseph I, and Charles VI, intrusion of imperial power in Church inner affairs caused concern. The climax was reached under Joseph II, when Pius VI was Pope.[12] The Austrian version of the essential elements of Febronianism is called Josephism.[13]

Maria Theresa of Austria had sixteen children, changed the family name to Hapsburg-Lorraine after marrying Francis of Lorraine, and took precautions for her heir not to repeat the chaos and grief which her own ascension to the Hapsburg Crown had caused.[14] She ensured that her husband became Emperor as Francis I. When he died in 1765, she secured the election of their first-born son, the strong-willed and eccentric Joseph, to be elected Emperor and also made him her co-regent. Mother and son clashed frequently until she died in 1780. Once Joseph II became sole ruler, there was no holding back to his plans or realization of his enlightened policies. One involved broadening a Church reform that some of his immediate predecessors had already attempted.

Josephism was not concerned with dogma but with the

---

[12] P. Levillain (ed.), "Pius VI"; *ODCC*, "Pius VI"; *CE*, "Pius VI."

[13] See R. Kann, *A History of the Hapsburg Empire, 1526-1918*, UCLA (1974); S.T. Myovich, *Josephism at its Boundaries*, UMI (1996); A. Wheatcroft, *The Hapsburgs*, Penguin (1996); op. cit.; Ingrao, op. cit.; Beales, Derek, op. cit.; Beales and Best, op. cit.; *CE*, "Josephism."

[14] See n. 36; B. Dawson, E. Derek, *Joseph II: In the Shadow of Maria Theresa, 1741-1780*, CUP (1987); R. Browning, *The War of the Austrian Succession*, Palgrave Macmillan (1995); Ingrao, op. cit.; Okey, op. cit.

subjection of the Catholic Church in the Hapsburg lands to the secular State. Maria Theresa and Joseph II considered themselves devout Catholics, but both also believed in firm State control over the Church. The empress made restrictions on religious holidays and prohibited the taking of religious vows before one's twenty-fourth birthday so as to improve the economy. She insisted that clerics be subject to the jurisdiction of the State in non-ecclesiastical matters and that the acquisition of land by the Church be controlled by the government.

Joseph II's most radical measures in matters of religion were the Edict of Tolerance of 1781, the Edict of Tolerance of 1782, and his monastic reforms.[15] The new legislation gave Lutherans, Calvinists, and Orthodox Christians close footing to Roman Catholics and allowed Jews to enter various trades and to study at universities. There was a fundamental difference between the policies of mother and son. While Maria Theresa regarded Protestants as heretics and Jews as the embodiment of the Antichrist, Joseph II respected other Christian faiths and believed Jews did good service for the State. In this regard, he was ahead of his time in acknowledging the dignity of all persons, though this was done on his own terms. He also toyed with the idea of setting up a national Austrian Catholic Church. Perceiving himself as enlightened, he tried to play emperor and pope.[16] He interfered directly in the inner life of the Catholic Church. His *fiat* dissolved those religious houses that he deemed superfluous, redrew boundaries of dioceses, abolished Church festivals and what he thought to be

---

[15] See C.R. Blitz, "The Religious Reforms of Joseph II (1780-1790) and the Economic Significance," *Journal of European Economic History*, 18 (1989) 583-586; R.C. Hochedlinger, *The Hapsburg Monarchy*, NY: St. Martin's Press (2001); A. Wheatcroft, op. cit.; Ingrao, op. cit.; Berenger, op. cit.

[16] In this regard, Joseph II was not very different from the later Byzantine Emperors who interfered in the inner life of the Orthodox Church.

superstitious veneration, and placed seminaries under state control. About a third of the Austrian religious houses ceased to exist and their patrimony was used toward the upkeep of existing parishes and to finance the establishment of new ones. He tried, without success, to simplify the Roman Catholic liturgy. He insisted that an episcopal candidate takes an oath of allegiance to the emperor before his episcopal ordination, and forbade bishops to have direct contact with Rome. Many of his religious policies were eventually discontinued, but the Edicts and the monastic reforms remained. Pius VI attempted to intervene personally by going to Vienna in 1782. The papal mission was a complete failure. In fact, after the Pope's departure, the emperor advocated more restriction on papal power. The Catholic Church in the imperial domains remained wealthy and influential but became completely subjugated to the secular State. When Joseph II returned the papal visit with one of his own to Rome in 1783, the Spanish embassy convinced him to abandon his project for a national Austrian Catholic Church. Once back in Austria, he found great resistance to his reforms from the majority of his Catholic subjects, including the clergy and the Archbishop of Vienna, the Hungarian and Belgian bishops, and the Austrian Netherlands. Ironically, he turned to Pius VI for assistance to convince the Belgian subjects not to revolt.

Grand-Duke Leopold of Tuscany, brother and successor of Joseph II as Holy Roman Emperor in 1790, attempted to apply Josephism in his domain. He was supported by Bishop Scipione de' Ricci of Pistoia, a Jansenist who adhered to Gallican principles. The two collaborated together to impose Josephism in the grand duchy through the Synod of Pistoia of 1786. The bishops, with two exceptions, resisted the execution of the synod's decrees. Pius VI condemned the synod in 1794, having already procured the resignation of Ricci in 1791.

---

## 10. Rome and the Chinese Rites Controversy

---

Missionary work with non-Christians has been a high priority in the Society of Jesus since the time of St. Ignatius of Loyola. By the year 1750, more than one-fifth of all Jesuits were involved in some kind of missionary activity.

The Jesuit China Mission began in the 1580's. At the time, the Chinese regarded their culture as the most advanced. They saw no need for new ideas or of any kind of foreign commerce. The Jesuits overcame this obstacle by sending their best scientists, particularly the astronomer Matteo Ricci, to the Chinese court.[17] They impressed the Chinese with their knowledge of astronomy and mechanics and became in effect in charge of the Imperial Observatory and much esteemed at the court. The Jesuits, in turn, were impressed with the Confucian elite, adapted their lifestyle, and began adjusting some liturgical and doctrinal aspects to the Confucian mentality, particularly veneration of ancestors, so as to gain converts. They argued the new approach, the so-called Chinese Rites, involved social and not religious ceremonies. But, they were denounced to Rome by both Franciscan and Dominican missionaries. It led to the so-called Chinese Rites Controversy and a final papal condemnation of such liturgical and doctrinal adaptations in 1742.

The imperial Ming Dynasty, established in 1368, began to crumble in the 1620s, leaving the country open to conquest by the Manchu, a "barbarian" people from beyond the Great Wall. The Manchu Qing Dynasty violently took power in 1644. Chaos was

---

[17] See J. Gernet, *China and the Christian Impact: A Conflict of Cultures*, J. Lloyd, (trans.), CUP (1985); S. Uhalley, Jr., X. Wu, (eds.), *China and Christianity: Burdened Past, Hopeful Future*, NY: M.E. Sharpe, Inc. (2001); Spiteri, *At Your Fingertips* III, nn. 38 (f), 60 (c).

supreme. It took the new conquerors some forty years to establish control over the Chinese peoples. Meanwhile, the elite Confucian scholars became demoralized and started questioning their very philosophy, eyeing in a better light the alternative Christian lifestyle presented by the Jesuits. Next, Emperor Kangxi issued an Edict of Toleration in 1692 whereby the Catholic Church was recognized as a faith not to be persecuted and the Chinese could openly practice Christianity. Thus, by the end of the seventeenth century, the Jesuits had many converts. Still, because the emperor progressively identified himself with the ancient Chinese customs and religious beliefs as serenity began to settle in the empire, he adopted mainstream Confucianism and gradually withdrew his support of religious toleration. Finally, his son, Emperor Yong-zheng, who was not pleased by Clement XI's papal decree of 1715 on Chinese Rites, banned Catholic missions from his empire in 1721.[18] By this time there were some one half million Chinese Catholics. Back in Rome, the Chinese Rites Controversy raged on until 1742 when Benedict XIV[19] definitively prohibited Chinese Catholics from participating in various Confucian rites.

---

[18] See S. Neill, *A History of Christian Missions,* Harmondsworth: Penguin Books (1964); D.J. Li, (trans.), *China in Transition,* NY: Van Nostrand Reinhold Company (1969).

[19] P. Levillain (ed.), "Benedict XIV"; *ODCC,* "Benedict XIV"; *CE,* "Benedict XIV."

# CHAPTER THREE

# Popes and Our Lady

## 11. Mariology

(a) Benedict XVI, when he was Cardinal Joseph Ratzinger and Prefect of the Congregation for the Doctrine of the Faith, granted an interview to Vittorio Messori in August 1984. He answered a series of questions regarding the state of the Church in the post-Vatican II era. The interview was subsequently published in 1985 in a book entitled *The Ratzinger Report*.[1] One set of questions dealt with the Blessed Virgin Mary. The Cardinal identified Our Lady as the cure for the current challenges and crises for the Church and the world. He very clearly affirmed the need of going back to Mary if one wants to return to the truth about Jesus Christ and about His Church.

(b) Mariology, a separate discipline from Christology, is a logical and necessary outcome of Christology. It is Christology developed to its full potential due to an unbreakable bond between Jesus and Mary. The two are very close but certainly not identical. Jesus Christ is truly God and truly man, while Mary is only human. As Cardinal Ratzinger stated in 1985, Mary contributes

---

[1] See Joseph Ratzinger, *The Ratzinger Report*, CA: Ignatius Press (1985).

to a fuller understanding of who Christ is and what He did.[2]

The term "Mariology" encompasses not only Catholic Marian theology, but also Mary's veneration, all aspects involving Marian devotion, and Marian art, music, and architecture throughout the entire Christian era. Mariology is both part of abstract doctrine and an important part of Church life. It is in a constant fluid state in that it continues to be developed by papal encyclicals, commentaries, the writings of Saints and Mariologists, the devotional life of the faithful, and down to the building of shrines on sites of Marian apparitions. Mariology is not simply a theological field studied by scholars, but a devotional concept embraced by hundreds of millions of Catholics who venerate Mary. It differs from other parts of theology in that its progress has quite often been driven from the grass roots level of the believing community and, at times, from private Marian apparitions, which, in turn, influence the higher levels of the Holy See as is the case in Lourdes and Fatima.[3]

There are four Marian dogmas.[4] These and other Marian teachings in the Catholic Church serve two functions. Marian dogmas present the Church's infallible teachings about Mary and her Son, highlighting the divine nature of Jesus Christ. On the other hand, Marian dogmas and other Church Marian teachings praise Mary and, through her, teach of God's graces given to her because she is the Mother of the Lord. Both functions underline

---

[2]  Cardinal Ratzinger, as Benedict XVI, reiterated this in his first reflection at the Synod of the Special Assembly for the Middle East (10-24 October 2010), while addressing the Synod Fathers on 11th October 2010.

[3]  See L. Gambero, *Mary and the Fathers of the Church: The Blessed Virgin Mary in Patristic Thought*, Ignatius Press (1999); *Mariology: A Guide for Priests, Deacons, Seminarians, and Consecrated Persons*, Goleta, CA: Seat of Wisdom Books (2007).

[4]  The four Marian dogmas are (a) Divine Motherhood, (2) Perpetual Virginity, (3) the Immaculate Conception of Mary and (4) Assumption into Heaven, body and soul.

the fact that Mary is who and what she is because of who Jesus Christ is.

(c) Numerous Saints and theological writers have focused on the uniquely distinct relationship between Mary and Jesus. Moreover, Popes, Ecumenical Councils, Doctors of the Church, and theological writers down the centuries have highlighted the inherent bond between Marian dogmas and teachings and the full acceptance of Christological dogmas and teachings.

Catholic Mariology goes back to the first century. The early Christians initially focused their piety on martyrs and subsequently they saw in Mary a bridge between the old and the new. St. Irenaeus[5] called Mary the "second Eve" because her cooperative obedience to God undid the harm that was rendered through Eve's disobedience. The earliest recorded prayer to Mary, *sub tuum praesidium* (under your protection), dates back to around 250. The First Council of Ephesus declared Mary as the *Theotokos* (God-bearer) in 431, implying that Jesus, Mary's Son, is truly God and man in one Person. The debate over the proper title for Mary was in fact a Christological question about the true nature of Jesus Christ, which was discussed in the subsequent Council of Chalcedon in 451. Roman Catholics, Old Catholics, Eastern Orthodox, Anglicans, and Lutherans affirm Mary as being the God-bearer. Furthermore, the teaching on the Assumption of Mary dates back to the Eastern Church of the fifth century.[6]

(d) The Protestant Reformers in the main objected to the

---

[5] See A. Robinson (trans.), *St. Irenaeus: The Demonstration of the Apostolic Preaching*, NY: Macmillan (1920); J. Pelikan, *The Christian Tradition: A History of the Development of Doctrine*, Vol. I, UCP (1975); idem., *Mary Through the Centuries: Her Place in the History of Culture*, YUP (1998).

[6] Pius XII, in 1950, declared as a dogma of the Roman Catholic Church the Assumption of Mary, body and soul, into heaven. Both Western and Eastern Christendom, since the sixth century, have celebrated this feast on 15th August.

devotional life of late medieval Catholicism, specifically to the many Marian devotions which had increased considerably as the Middle Ages was nearing its end. The Marian devotions intensified when Western Europe was threatened by the expansionist program of the Moslem Ottoman Turks in the later part of the fifteenth century. Mary, above any other Saint, was seen by the common people as their unique protector during such adversarial and frightening times. The central and singular role of Jesus Christ in redemption became somewhat overshadowed. By the eve of the Reformation, Mary was perceived as having great influence on earth and in heaven. One could mistakenly claim that Mary was worshipped rather than venerated. Of course, the Catholic Church always maintained that worship belongs to God alone and the worship of any other than God, including Mary, is idolatry. But the common man was not a theologian and generally illiterate and failed to make the essential distinction between worshipping God alone and venerating the Saints, including Mary. In any case, Marian devotion gradually disappeared from Protestant liturgical practices within one hundred years of the Reformation. On the other hand, the Catholic Church provided a strong defense of her Marian theology and practices, institutionalizing some Marian devotions, such as the Feast of Our Lady of the Rosary in 1572.

(e) On the eve of the Protestant Reformation in Germany, the Virgin Mary was the most frequently depicted and invoked Saint. Late medieval Germany had numerous shrines, altarpieces, statues and images dedicated in her honor, while devotional literature and sermons made frequent references to her. But humanists like Erasmus criticized some excessive Marian devotions, especially pilgrimages. Luther took this a step further by condemning the late medieval Church for allotting Mary too prominent a role in the redemptive process. He stated that man was saved by God's grace alone and the intercession of Saints, including Mary, was empty. Marian devotion was relegated to the level of superstition and idolatry. However, given Mary's role in the Bible, she could never be erased altogether from Protestant piety. The transformation of the role of Mary in Lutheranism was gradual because Germany was full of Marian images and traditions. The role of Mary and even some non-scriptural scenes from her life and the Feast of the Assumption were tolerated in Nuremberg on the tenuous grounds that they were popular. In fact, Catholic and Protestant devotional practices stayed rather fluid and adaptable, depending on the current social and political situation in a specific area.

It was an altogether different story in Augsburg, a city dominated by the more radical south-west German and Swiss Reformed theology. Zwingli hotly condemned the invocation of Saints, including Mary. Marian feasts were summarily dismissed and officially sponsored iconoclasm was undertaken. However, since the Peace of Augsburg in 1555 bestowed legal and official recognition to Catholicism and Lutheranism alone[7] and rendered Augsburg a bi-confessional city, Zwinglian zeal was reduced because that brand of creed was not recognized in said Peace.

(f) All of the original leaders of the Protestant Reformation had been raised Roman Catholic and were exposed to Marian and other kinds of devotions at a certain stage in their upbringing. Consequently, up to a point, they had been exposed to Marian devotion which, in turn, influenced their reaction to this kind of popular spirituality. Mary also became an important confessional symbol in Augsburg and Marian devotion became a powerful symbol of the Counter-Reformation, polarizing the city's

---

[7] See Spiteri, *At Your Fingertips* III, n. 40 (b).

inhabitants. Some Catholic Marian depictions portrayed Mary as triumphant over heretics, while Protestants usually blamed the "devil-inspired" Jesuits for adding the non-biblical intercessory invocation in the "Hail Mary." In due course, Marian piety formed an important part of the Counter-Reformation's conversion program in Augsburg.

---

## 12. Roman Catholic Mariology

(a) Protestants generally claim that Mariology has its roots in the Middle Ages, oblivious of the fact that it goes back to the early Church. However, the medieval period witnessed a substantial growth and development of Mariology, and Marian hymns became staples of monastic plainsong. Devotional practices also grew in number and from the year 1000 onward more churches, including many of Europe's greatest cathedrals, were dedicated to Mary. During this era, Blessed John Duns Scotus argued for Mary's Immaculate Conception, depicting it as the most perfect form of redemption possible by a unique divine act.[8] Different Popes during the Middle Ages published decrees and authorized feasts and processions in honor of Mary. The recitation of different versions of the rosary became very popular. Moreover, Renaissance artists had a superabundant depiction of Mary. To mention a few, there were Alberti, Fra Angelico, Filippo Lippi, Giotto, Botticelli, Andrea del Castagno, Pisanello, Signorelli, Ghirlandaio, Bellegambe, Bosch, David, Dürer, the two Holbeins, Fouquet, the Clouets, d'Eyck, Hey, Bru Juan de Flandes, Huguet, and de San Leocadio.

---

[8] Blessed Pius IX, in 1854, defined as Catholic dogma the Immaculate Conception of Mary.

The Catholic Church, during the Reformation and at the Council of Trent, defended its Marian teachings against Protestant views. A few years later, the Catholic forces' victory against the Turks at Lepanto was attributed to Mary's intercession and was followed by a significant resurgence of Marian devotions, focusing especially on Our Lady as Queen of Heaven and Earth and on her role as intercessor of many graces.

During the Baroque period there were lasting Marian impressions in classical music, painting, and architecture, and in numerous Marian shrines in Spain, France, Italy, Austria, Bavaria, and South America. Literature on Mary became voluminous. Many renowned theologians contributed to this literature, in particular Francisco Suárez, Sts. Robert Bellarmine, Laurence of Brindisi, and Francis de Sales. Sts. John Eudes and Louis de Montfort vigorously defended the Catholic Marian teachings against the often anti-Marian Jansenists. Diverse Popes spoke and wrote in praise of Mary. Alexander VII, in 1661, declared that the soul of Mary was free from original sin; Clement XI extended the Feast of the Immaculate Conception for the whole Church in 1708[9] and established the Feast of the Rosary in 1716; Benedict XIII established the Feast of the Seven Sorrows in 1727; and Benedict XIV gave public support of the Angelus prayer in 1742. Popular Marian piety became entrenched with numerous Marian pilgrimages, Salve devotions, litanies, processions, theater plays, and hymns. Marian fraternities had millions of members.

(b) The Enlightenment put great emphasis on scientific progress and rationalism. Catholic theology went often on the defensive and this had some adverse effects on Mariology. Marian theology was dropped in some seminaries, such as that of Salzburg

---

[9]   The dogma of the Immaculate Conception of Mary would be defined in 1854.

in 1782. Popular Marian devotion lessened, pilgrimages to Marian shrines were significantly reduced, and some theologians went so far as to call for the abolition of all Marian feast days except for those with biblical foundations and the ancient feast of the Assumption. Many Marian devotional sites or shrines were shut down or pilgrims were drastically reduced in number due to the closure of many monasteries. On the other hand, many Benedictines, Jesuits, Carmelites, and Franciscans, along with many lay members of Marian fraternities, resisted these anti-Marian trends.[10] St. Alphonsus Maria Liguori put pen to paper and wrote numerous beautiful and popular Marian reflections and prayers, the most popular of which was the book, *The Glories of Mary*, that repeated the medieval idea that Christ is the king of justice, while Mary is the mother of mercy. The religious congregation he founded, the Redemptorists, continued his promotion of Marian devotions. Yet, during the Enlightenment, Mariology lost much although the basics were kept and served as a basis for the Marian development during the nineteenth century.

---

## 13. Early Protestant View on Mary

Protestant views of Mary were as diverse as the numerous versions of Protestant theologies of the time. Luther, Calvin, and Zwingli, in their respective writings, expressed some residual Marian piety, but the Protestant emphasis on *sola scriptura* led to a rather unique Protestant view of Mary.

Luther rejected the intercession of Mary and every Saint

---

[10] Popular devotions were confined to the Italian Peninsula, Spain, Poland, Malta and a few other places untouched by the general European currents of thought.

but, at the same time, spoke of Mary as being both a symbol of the goodness of God and a special inspirational woman of faith. Apart from his harsh criticism of the veneration of Mary, he accepted the Marian decrees of the Ecumenical Councils and the Marian dogmas, thereby upholding her Perpetual Virginity and being the Mother of God. He initially accepted the Immaculate Conception, though later he modified his views and taught that Mary was only devoid of sin throughout her life. He wrote that the New Testament stated nothing about the Assumption of Mary, but he emphasized the fact that Mary and the Saints abide with God. He maintained that Mary was the consummate recipient of God's grace and the supreme model of Christian virtues for she had a special relationship to Christ, being the *Theotokos*, the God-bearer.

Calvin taught that because God chose Mary to be the Mother of His Son, she should receive the highest honor. He accepted Mary's perpetual virginity and claimed that he was a true follower of Mary because he freed her from all the misuse of titles and honors that belong solely to her Son. He expressed much concern about the title of "Mother of God" given to Mary by the Council of Ephesus and stated that all Marian titles and honors promoted by the Catholic Church were frivolous and blasphemous.

Zwingli stated that the more a person's honor and love for Christ increases, then more respect is due to Mary for she was a very unique, holy, chaste, and sinless woman whom God chose to be the Mother of His Son.

# Popes Dealing with Nations

# CHAPTER FOUR

# Diplomatic Relations

## 14. Concordats

(a) A *concordat* may be generally defined as a legal device by which the Holy See, representing the Universal Catholic Church,[1] and a specific civil State agree to regulate certain specific matters of mutual or individual interests, using as their basis a common contractual and normative approach. International law, common law, civil law and Church (canon) law claim the concordat as a part of their respective fields.[2] Concordats, for many centuries, have been part of the history of the Catholic Church in its struggle to affirm its proper freedom and independence from civil governments and maintain religious autonomy. As an engagement between the Holy See and a sovereign State, the concordat assumes a unique position in Church, international and national affairs. Since the end of World War I, concordats have been drawn in the form of international treaties, have been accepted as international diplomatic documents, and their number has increased dramatically. As in the case of international treaties, negotiations and signatures

---

[1]  The Holy See is the organ through which the Catholic Church acts in her international relations.

[2]  See L.J. Spiteri, *Concordat Provisions*, Washington, DC: CUA (1992).

and ratification by both the Holy See and a specific State are the three phases through which concordats have to pass in order to become effective law. The form in which such agreements appear, however, has changed down the centuries.

The North African Pope St. Gelasius I[3] was an expert in Church-State relations. While personal secretary of St. Felix III, whom he succeeded as Pope, he wrote a letter to the Roman Emperor Zeno in 488 in which he pointed out that an emperor is not the lord but the son of the Catholic Church through baptism. Subsequently, in 495, the Pope had occasion to formulate his thesis of the relations between spiritual and political powers. He stated that while emperors are subject to bishops in spiritual matters by virtue of baptism, bishops are subject to emperors in secular matters. This thesis established the Gelasian Theory of the Two Swords. Some Popes in the Middle Ages argued that the spiritual and secular powers were rooted in the social body of Christianity because an individual was simultaneously a son of the Church and a member of the civil State. But, there was always great tension between Rome, the residence of the Popes, and Constantinople, the residence of the Roman Emperors, and later on between Popes and Holy Roman Emperors, particularly captured in the Investiture Controversy.[4]

(b) The Catholic Church began utilizing concordats with the disintegration of Constantine's Caesaro-Papism in 1122. That year Blessed Callixtus II[5] and Holy Roman Emperor Henry V entered into the Concordat of Worms which brought to an end the long Investiture Controversy in the empire. There were other

---

[3]  P. Levillain (ed.), "Gelasius I," op. cit.; Kelly, "Gelasius I," op. cit.
[4]  See Spiteri, *At Your Fingertips* I, n. 29.
[5]  P. Levillain (ed.), "Callixtus II," op. cit.; *ODCC*, "Callixtus II," op. cit.; Spiteri, *At Your Fingertips* I, 29 (c).

similar concordats on the Investiture Controversy following that of Worms.[6] A concordat appeared in the form of two individual declarations, issued by each party respectively, stating their consent to the matters and terms agreed upon. This form remained in almost constant use during the following eight centuries, that is, until the beginning of the nineteenth century when another *modus procedendi* (way of doing things) was introduced as another form of treaty, especially in relation to non-Catholic States. However, there have been and remain other forms of agreements concluded between the Holy See and civil States, such as *accords, protocols,* and *modus vivendi*. Nevertheless, while the latter documents are undoubtedly diplomatic instruments, they either lack the solemnity and range of concordats or they concern the interpretation of existing agreements or matters of lesser importance.

One might be tempted to conclude that concordats lack anything spiritual. This is far from being the case! A concordat is an agreement between two fundamentally distinct and different powers. The State is always a legal entity which is lay, can be Catholic or non-Catholic or atheistic or totalitarian or socialistic, and so forth. Yet, despite past claims by secular sovereigns that they (allegedly) ruled by divine right, a civil State is never divinely instituted as is the case with the Catholic Church. One has simply to recall the fact that down the centuries, while royal houses have been replaced or abolished, or countries have disappeared, or new countries have appeared, the Catholic Church has been constantly in existence since its institution by Jesus Christ.

---

6   For example, there was a concordat between King Dinis of Portugal and the bishops of Portugal in 1289, which was ratified by Pope Nicholas IV. It should be noted that the 'Concordat of London' of 1107 between Henry I of England and the Bishops of England under the leadership of St. Anselm had suggested a comprise of how to end the Investiture Controversy. The suggestion was taken up at the Concordat of Worms.

Though the Catholic Church is also a legal entity, she is much more than this for she is also the presence of Jesus Christ in the world. Furthermore, since a concordat is a means of participation in the life of the Church, it is also one of its spiritual works. The ultimate aim of a concordat is the presence of the Church in the life of people, citizens and not, in a specific secular State. As a recognized international legal entity, the Holy See, representing the Universal Catholic Church, is able to enter into treaties and to initiate relations even with those civil States in which the Catholic Faith is sprouting or officially non-existent.

A concordat, like any international treaty, limits the exercise of the sovereignty of the State as well as protects it. It is one of the means which limits and safeguards contemporary exigencies of the two orders, the religious and the political, and can be a point of encounter for a fruitful collaboration between the Church and secular States. History has proven that the limits of the competence of each of these two spheres can be elastic as well as problematic for interests are intermingled with rights. A concordat is a point of departure in that it poses the fundamental principle for reciprocal trust. It outlines the direction of Church-State cooperation, determining norms which will be transformed on the internal level of each contracting party to be followed and executed authentically and scrupulously. It calls for an ongoing dialogue on the level of the supreme authorities of Church and State.

---

### 15. Church-State Relations

(a) Once the distinction was made between the respective competence of the Catholic Church and the civil State, there emerged a number of theories. For example, the "theocratic" held that since

Christ has all heavenly and earthly power, the Pope, being Christ's Vicar on earth, enjoyed all power. It was argued that the Pope, then, transmitted royal power to secular sovereigns. The theory was based on St. Augustine's teachings on the Two Cities. Popes in the Middle Ages advocated this theory. Absolute papal power was especially advanced by Gregory VII, Innocent III, and the 1302 papal bull, *Unam Sanctam*, of Boniface VIII.[7] This claim brought the Catholic Church a lot of grief.

On the other hand, there are basically three different legal systems which have regulated and regulate the relationship between the Church and secular States down the centuries. Each system presupposes different concepts of the nature of the Church and the secular State. The Church teaches about its own nature, its rights as received from Jesus Christ, and its unalterable character. The Church also speaks about the nature of the State. Yet, because historic reality affects Church-State relationships, the order of theory and the order of practice must be always distinguished. Therefore, since the Church exists in the world, it may adapt to world political situations, utilizing every opportunity offered by civil States.

(b) As the united Western Christendom became shattered through the Protestant Reformation, the Church and different civil governments tried to find some solutions to bring order to a chaotic Western society. The Church tried to uphold and protect the rights of its members and its own autonomy in Protestant States, as well as curtail the interference by civil authorities which, Catholic or not, also wanted to control, if not eliminate, Church involvement in their political life. Concordats became one of the effective diplomatic means to foster satisfactory Church-State relations. Though the Church and the State were fundamentally

---

[7] P. Levillain (ed.), "Boniface VIII," op. cit.; *ODCC*, "Boniface VIII," op. cit.

distinct powers in their origins and aims, the two institutions met in the sphere of international relationship.

(c) The Confessional State embraces, supports, and protects a given Church, Catholic or otherwise. This happens when there is an official religion of a State. This system dates back to the Diet of Augsburg of 1555 through which Charles V, in an effort to end the wars that ensued principally in Germany as a result of the Reformation, tried to find a peaceful solution between his German Catholic and Protestant subjects. The Diet initiated the idea of the Confessional State. In essence, the unhappy solution was that the religion of the subjects was that of their ruler. Subsequently, the Church entered into different concordats with different Confessional States, be they Catholic or non-Catholic.

(ii) The Separatist State insists on complete separation of Church and State. A civil State can be either hostile or indifferent to a creed in particular or to all creeds. This kind of State acts always in terms of laicism. The hostile State is always antagonistic to all creeds, and although it can prohibit public and private worship, it usually relegates religious activity to a private affair. On the other hand, an indifferent State ignores religious activity while respecting the autonomy of all religions and insists on the complete autonomy of the State. This relationship allows for a quasi-complete separation between Church and State in which the Church is treated as a corporation of public law and as such is recognized and assisted by the State.

(iii) The Lay or Secular State falls between the Confessional State and the Separatist State. It claims incompetence to intrude into religious matters, thereby maintaining neutrality. It respects and even favors all the religions of its citizens inasmuch as these religions promote the common good, which is also the end and purpose of the State.

## 16. Selection of Bishops

The selection of a bishop has always been one of the most important acts in the life of the Catholic Church. The history of the Church in the West points out that there have been various methods used for the nomination and selection of episcopal candidates. The selection of bishops in the first six centuries, with very few variations, was made by the clergy and laity and the one chosen was consecrated by the provincial bishops with the consent of the metropolitan bishop.[8] This method was replaced in the Middle Ages with the nomination being made by the cathedral chapters of canons.[9] By the mid-thirteenth century, the confirmation of the bishop-elect was already reserved to Rome. Yet, although a cathedral chapter of canons formally elected a bishop, there was much interference from royal houses. The abuse can be traced back to the fourth century when, upon the death of Pope Liberius in 366, two factions in Rome elected their own candidate as Bishop of Rome. It led to a bloody strife between the two parties. Valentinian I, Roman Emperor of the West, opted for (St.) Damasus. The act unwittingly gave the Emperor the final say in the appointment of the Bishop of Rome. When St. Damasus died in 384, the clergy and populace of Rome sought the opinion of Valentinian II about the election of (St.) Siricius as the new Bishop of Rome. These two instances of the involvement of civil rulers in the See of Rome were a foreshadowing of what was to occur frequently in episcopal elections from the fifth century onward, and in papal conclaves until 1903.

---

[8] See J. Lynch, "Co-responsibility in the First Five Centuries: Presbyteral Colleges and the Election of Bishops," *The Jurist* 31 (1971).

[9] See R.L. Benson, "Election by Community and Chapter: Reflections on Co-Responsibility in the Historical Church," *The Jurist* 31 (1971).

Around the year 480 the *Statuta ecclesiae antique*[10] of Gaul enshrined the long-term formula of episcopal elections for the West that would last till the Middle Ages. The election was done by the consent of the clergy and the laity in the presence of the bishops of the area, the metropolitan archbishop and the civil authorities.

On the other hand, in the Eastern Roman Empire, the Church historian Socrates of Constantinople attacked the Eastern Emperor Theodosius II in 435 for attempting to interfere with episcopal elections.[11] Yet, shortly thereafter the emperors, perceiving themselves to be the embodiment of law on earth, began issuing their ecclesiastical laws, called *nomocanons*, and appointing many bishops. One of the more celebrated imperial appointments was that of Patriarch Photius of Constantinople in 858 by Emperor Michael II after the latter deposed Ignatius as Patriarch of Constantinople. Pope Nicholas I was involved in the subsequent controversy.

The West, too, had its own struggle in coming to terms with the role of civil authorities in episcopal elections. St. Gregory the Great advocated that the preference of secular rulers should be taken into account during episcopal elections for pragmatic reasons. When he was elected Pope, the land was devastated by floods, famine, the plague, and the Lombard invasion from the north. It was a period of great unrest in Western Europe. Hence, the Pope sought to get on his side the new rulers in Italy, Spain, and Gaul by making concessions, one being that of a serious role for a prince in episcopal elections. In turn, he expected the newly established royalty to help him withstand the threats from Byzantium.

---

[10] The Statutes of the Ancient Church.
[11] Socrates was reiterating Canon 12 of the Council of Laodicaea of 366 which even excluded the laity from episcopal elections. The emperor was a lay person.

Perhaps an encapsulation of the abuse of princely preroga-
tive may be found in canon 25 of the Council of Toledo XII in
681. Having established the primacy of Toledo,[12] the primate was
directed to ordain as bishop the one whom the king had chosen.
Thus, the wish of the king enjoyed the decisive role. The abuse
eventually became entangled with the Investiture Controversy.

Meanwhile, appeals to Popes over episcopal appointments
continued to be submitted even when they resided in Avignon.
In time, after many intriguing difficulties with episcopal elections, Urban V decreed in 1383 that the Roman Pontiff had the
exclusive and ultimate right against the right of the clergy and
civil authorities in the nomination of bishops. This policy lasted
until the end of the Middle Ages. Next, Popes began explicitly
granting permission to rulers to approve or name episcopal candidates, usually through some provision in a concordat. Thus,
for example, in the 1516 Concordat of Bologna between Francis
I of France and Leo X, the Pope explicitly granted the King the
right to name bishops. This right would be reiterated in the 1801
Concordat between Pius VII and Napoleon Bonaparte.[13]

---

## 17. The Padroado of Portugal

---

Portugal became an empire in the sixteenth century. The Catholic
Church had to rely especially on Portugal and Spain to propagate
the faith beyond the European world since these two empires
had vast colonies overseas, were staunch Catholic countries, their

---

[12] Toledo remains the Primatial See in Spain in our time.
[13] Nowadays, the French president still enjoys the privilege in the appointment of
the Bishops for the archdiocese of Strasbourg and the diocese of Metz.

sovereigns were interested in their new subjects converting to Catholicism, and the respective sovereigns provided transportation to missionaries. However, the monarchs also expected that their political agenda be promoted not only by their royal representatives in their colonies but also by Catholic missionaries.

Portugal, like the Holy Roman Empire, France and Spain, has a long history of signing concordats with the Church. Initially concordats with Portugal were enacted in one of two ways. One method entailed the ratification by the Pope of a treaty between the Portuguese Crown and one or more bishops in Portugal. This had a partial regional effect. The second method was a concordat between the Holy See and the Portuguese Crown. This had amplified effects.

The first recorded treaty between the Portuguese Crown and a bishop in Portugal was that of Sancho I of Portugal, and Bishop Martinho II Rodrigues of Porto. It was ratified by Innocent III in 1210. Other similar treaties followed. Conversely, the first concordat with Portugal was between St. Gregory IX and Sancho II in 1238. It initiated the Portuguese Padroado, in which the Holy See delegated to the Portuguese Crown the administration of the Church within the kingdom.

Once Portugal became an empire, the Holy See allowed it to expand the Padroado privileges to its colonies, beginning with the 1454 Concordat. But, there was always an underlying tension between the Portuguese Crown, on the one hand, and the Holy See and the Bishops of Portugal and its colonies, on the other, especially when it pertained to appointing men to high Church offices. This came to a head during the reign of João V in the seventeenth century. The Holy See grew weary of the political intrigues that the Portuguese Crown exercised in manipulating the election of bishops. Two centuries of tension was somewhat diminished with the 1857 Concordat between Blessed Pius IX and Pedro V in which Portugal was given the right to nominate a bishop and then present the one name for confirmation by the Holy See.

## 18. Concordats during the Eighteenth Century

A number of Popes signed concordats during the eighteenth century. Benedict XIII and Victor Amadeus II of Sardinia, in 1727, confirmed the House of Savoy's right to nominate candidates to ecclesiastical offices. Clement XII and Augustus II of Poland signed a concordat in 1736. The following year, 1737, the same Pope made a concordat with Philip V of Spain. Benedict XIV signed a number of concordats. He signed concordats with Charles Emmanuel II of Sardinia, respectively in 1741, 1742 and 1750, in an attempt to resolve the issue of who was the actual overlord of that island because centuries earlier a Pope had given the island to the King of Spain as a fiefdom. Benedict XIV also signed a concordat with Charles II of the Two Sicilies in 1741, with Ferdinand VI of Spain in 1753, and with Maria Theresa of Austria regarding the Duchy of Milan in 1757. Clement XIV and Charles Emmanuel III signed a concordat in 1770. Pius VI signed a concordat with Maria I of Portugal in 1778 and one with Joseph II of Austria in 1784, which dealt with Austria's right to nominate the bishops of Milan and Mantua.

## 19. Concordats during the Nineteenth Century

A number of concordats were signed in the nineteenth century. The most renowned was the 1801 Concordat between Pius VII and Napoleon Bonaparte. Though the concordat was lop-sided toward France, it helped to eliminate the confusion that had beleaguered the French Catholic clergy since the enactment of the Civil Constitution of the Clergy in 1790 which had rendered the Church as a department of the French State. The provisions of this concordat stayed essentially in effect until 1905. The 1817 Concordat between the Holy See and the restored Louis XVIII of France never went into effect.

Napoleon, at the Peace of Lunéville in 1801, reconstructed the German States by annexing to France those lands which were situated on the left bank of the Rhine and uniting the rest into the Rhine Federation. He compensated the dispossessed German princes by giving them secularized Church lands, despite Pius VII's useless protests. The Catholic Church in Germany had to be reorganized. Bavaria opened negotiations with Rome for a Concordat. Other German States followed suit. But the Pope preferred to deal with Francis II of Austria instead of dealing with each individual German State. After the suppression of the Holy Roman Empire in 1806, Napoleon aimed, but failed, to enter into a uniform Concordat for the Rhine Federation. Following his fall, Rome entered into separate Concordats with each German State, the first being with Bavaria in 1817.

Pius VII and England had grown closer together because of their common opposition and resistance to Napoleon. There was talk of an accord between them regarding the predicament of the Catholic Church in Ireland. But the Irish hierarchy was so vehemently opposed to the project that nothing came out of it.[14]

Belgium and the Netherlands, under William I, entered into a Concordat with Leo XII in 1827.[15] Russia signed a Concordat in 1847, and Haiti in 1861. Many of the newly independent South American countries respectively signed Concordats with the Holy See: Guatemala and Costa Rica in 1852; Honduras and Nicaragua in 1861; San Salvador, Venezuela, and Ecuador in 1862; the 1862 Concordat with Ecuador was updated in 1881;[16] the Dominican Republic and a revised one with Guatemala, both in 1884; Colombia in 1887, with many supplements beginning in 1892; and a new Concordat with Ecuador in 1890.

---

[14] See M. Cronin, *A History of Ireland*, Palgrave Macmillan (2003); M. McAuliffe, K. O'Donnell and L. Lane (eds.), *Advances in Irish History*, Palgrave Macmillan (2009).

[15] The Concordat ceased when Belgium and the Netherlands were permanently separated in 1831.

[16] The Concordat was suspended in 1887.

# CHAPTER FIVE

# Rome and Paris

## 20. Popes and Louis XIV

(a) The pontificate of Innocent X was a mixed bag in papal foreign policy. He was elected Pope during the devastating Thirty Years War[1] and became entangled in a number of political issues that involved France. He almost caused a war between the Papal States and France at the beginning of his pontificate when he initiated legal proceedings against two Barberini Cardinals, nephews of the deceased Urban VIII, charging them with misappropriation and abuse of public funds. They sought refuge in France under the protection of Cardinal Mazarin. The tension was eventually defused and Rome and Paris established peace between them.[2] However, Mazarin arrested and imprisoned Jean Francois Paul de Gondi, Cardinal de Retz in 1652, accusing him of being an instigator of the Fronde Revolt.[3] Mazarin ignored the Pope's protests against a violent act against a Cardinal. When Retz escaped from Nantes in 1654, the Pope gave him shelter. Furthermore,

---

[1]  See R.G. Asch, *The Thirty Years War: The Holy Roman Empire and Europe, 1618-48*, Palgrave Macmillan (1997); G. Parker (ed.), *The Thirty Years War*, Routledge (1997); R. Bonney, *The Thirty Years War: 1618-1649*, Osprey Publications (2002); Spiteri, *At Your Fingertips* III, nn. 52, 58.

[2]  See Spiteri, *At Your Fingertips* III, n. 19 (e).

[3]  See Spiteri, *At Your Fingertips* III, n. 20 (b).

despite the objections of Mazarin and the exiled Queen Henrietta Marie of England, the Pope sided with the Irish Catholics and assisted them with both military equipment and money during the English Civil War. The Irish Catholics would pay a very heavy price because Oliver Cromwell began a practical systematic genocide of them.

(b) The foreign policy of Alexander VII, a seasoned diplomat, left much to be desired, for he ironically disliked State affairs. His pontificate was marred with the ongoing friction between the Pope and Cardinal Mazarin, who had openly opposed him during the negotiations at the Peace of Westphalia, upheld the prerogatives of the Gallican Church, and was openly against him during the conclave. Though Mazarin had to swallow his pride and accept Chigi as Pope, he continued his hostilities by convincing Louis XIV not to send the usual embassy of obedience to the new Pope, foiled the appointment of a French ambassador to Rome, had diplomatic affairs conducted by Cardinal Protectors who were personal enemies of the Pope, and finally sent the equally hostile Duc de Crequi as ambassador to Rome. The latter precipitated a quarrel between France and the Papacy that resulted in Rome's temporary loss of Avignon and the Pope's forced acceptance of the humiliating Treaty of Pisa in 1664. On the other hand, Clement IX's foreign policy met some minor success. He managed to provide a temporary accommodation between the Holy See and the French prelates who refused to join in condemning Jansenism, the *Pax Clementina*. He served as mediator at the Peace of Aachen in 1668, trying to resolve the issue that led to the War of the Spanish Succession.[4] Neither did he shy away from gravely admonishing the ambitious Louis XIV of France against the aggressive policy he was establishing in Europe.

---

[4]   See n. 41.

(c) Blessed Innocent XI's relationship with Louis XIV validated the reasons why the king opposed his election as Pope. Innocent XI continuously and futilely insisted on Papal Primacy while the absolute Louis XIV extended his regal power and carried out his Gallican policies. The king convoked an Assembly of the French Clergy in 1682. It adopted the four articles known as the Gallican Liberties which, in effect, annulled Papal Primacy. The Pope responded by declaring them null and stated he would never allow any of the assembly's participants to become bishops. When the king realized the Pope meant business, he tried to appease him by revoking the Edict of Nantes in 1685 and initiating a persecution of Huguenots. The Pope was displeased with the king's extreme measures and continued to withhold episcopal confirmations. He also annulled the right of sanctuary at the embassies in Rome for criminals sought by the papal court. He then notified the new French ambassador, Marquis de Lavardin, that he would not be recognized as ambassador in Rome unless he renounced this right. But Louis XIV would not give it up. After Lavardin entered Rome in November 1687 with a French army, forcibly taking possession of his palace, the Pope treated him as excommunicate. The Church for the French in Rome, St. Louis of France, was placed under interdict.

The tension between Innocent XI and Louis XIV intensified in 1688 by the Pope's decision to fill the vacant archiepiscopal see of Cologne, whose occupant was also a Prince-Elector and, thus, directly involved in north-western German affairs. Louis XIV wanted Cardinal William Egon of Fürstenberg, then Bishop of Strasbourg, to be the new archbishop and, thus, Elector of Cologne. On the other hand, Emperor Leopold I and the rest of Europe wanted Joseph Clement von Wittelsbach as the archbishop. If Egon became the archbishop, it meant that France would gain a significant say in German affairs. The college of canons of the cathedral of Cologne had the right to elect the new archbishop. When neither candidate received the necessary votes, the Pope appointed Wittelsbach. Louis XIV's retaliation[5] was one of the causes that triggered the Nine Years War, often called the War of the Grand Alliance because it involved a coalition among Emperor Leopold I, William III of England, Charles II of Spain, Victor Amadeus II of Savoy and most of the princes of the Holy Roman Empire, all of these united against Louis XIV. The war was fought primarily on the European continent and its seas. At one stage Ireland served as one of its theaters in the battles between King James II and his son-in-law, King William III, both of England. There were also battles between the French and British settlers and their respective Native American allies in colonial North America. France ended in defeat, but was not discouraged for long.

## 21. Popes and Louis XV

(a) Clement XI's ineptitude soon became evident after his papal election. He had originally favored the French Duke Philip of Anjou, grandson of Louis XIV, as the heir to Charles II of Spain. Thus, he evoked the ire of Emperor Leopold II and subsequently that of his successor, Joseph I, who invaded the Papal States. The Pope, for all practical purposes, became a non-entity among the Catholic European Crowns. Yet, he played a crucial role in sub-

---

[5] Louis XIV retaliated by occupying the papal territory of Avignon, imprisoning the papal nuncio, appealing to a General Council and hinting that he would establish the Church in France as an independent church from Rome. The matter was settled in favor of Rome soon after the death of the Pope.

jugating Jansenism in France, though this was carried out due to Louis XIV's national political policy. He condemned Jansenism in July 1705.[6] Subsequently, in 1708, he condemned the *Réflections morales* of Pasquier Quesnel for their Jansenist roots. In addition, in September 1713, he published the Papal Bull, *Unigenitus*, which condemned 101 propositions extracted from Quesnel's writings. After the death of Louis XIV in 1715, the Jansenist leaders appealed for a general council. The Pope stood firm and in August 1718 excommunicated all those who had appealed for a general council. Meanwhile, France was very careful in enacting only those sections of *Unigenitus* which did not touch on the traditional liberties of the Gallican Church. France used the Papacy to get what it wanted and without sacrificing any of its claims and control over the Church in France.

(b) The relationship between France and Innocent XIII was based on a give-and-take model, though the Pope gave more than he took. He appeased the Regent of France, Philip II of Orleans,[7] by creating Cardinal the corrupt French Prime Minister Archbishop Guillaume Dubois. Conversely, the Jansenists, in 1721, aware of the Pope's aversion toward the Jesuits, asked that he revoke Clement XI's condemnation of Jansenism. Instead, the Pope wrote to the Regent of France, reaffirmed the condemnation, and asked that the Crown actively discipline Jansenist bishops. Perhaps the Pope did not fully realize that his request gave more credence to France's Gallican Liberties.

The noble Roman Orsini family had provided the Church

---

[6] See n. 6.

[7] Philip II of Orleans was regent of France from 1715 until his death in 1723 due to King Louis XV's minority. Louis XV became king at age 5, succeeding his great-grandfather in 1715.

with three Popes: Celestine III,[8] Nicholas III, and Benedict XIII. The latter was elected after a nine week conclave which witnessed the interference of Catholic Crowns, including France which, like the Hapsburgs and the Bourbons, thought he would be a neutral Pope for he lacked political experience. But he stood firm in his total condemnation of Jansenism and, through the avid partici- pation of the Roman Curia, secured the submission to all the provisions of *Unigenitus* from the subtle Jansenist Archbishop of Paris, Cardinal Louis-Antoine de Noailles in 1728. On the other hand, Benedict XIV had a pastoral approach toward Jansenists. Adopting the middle ground, he decreed that only those who publicly refuted the provisions of *Unigenitus* could be denied Holy Communion. Yet, the prestige of the Holy See kept going further down during his pontificate. He was either bullied or many times simply ignored despite the fact that he had entered into a number of concordats with diverse European Catholic Crowns.

    (c) Concordats at this time served more as a justification by secular States to exert more control over the Church within their respective realms. Still, there were a few instances when Benedict XIV stuck to his guns as was the case when, despite adverse pressure from the Bourbon Crowns, he recognized the consort of Empress Maria Theresa, Francis I, as the new Holy Roman Emperor in 1745. France, in this instance, lost a round in the power-struggle game with the Holy See. It made sure that no rounds were lost during the next pontificate. The Parliament of Paris, supported by members of the Enlightenment, passed a resolution for the suppression of the Society of Jesus in France

---

[8]   Celestine III was already 85 years old when he was elected Pope in 1191. He tried to resign the papacy toward the end of his life and designated the Benedictine Cardinal Giovanni di San Paolo to succeed him. The Cardinals outrightly refused his request.

in 1762. When the Pope declared null the Paris parliamentary resolution, the French Crown reacted by reaffirming its Gallican Liberties and expelling the Jesuits in November 1764. In turn, the Bourbon Crowns in southern Europe formed a united front and demanded the papal suppression of the Society of Jesus. When the Bourbons were censured on Holy Thursday 1768, there was an adverse reaction, with France occupying the papal territories of Avignon and Venaissin. Clement XIII died before more abuse could be hurled upon him. What the Catholic Crowns could not squeeze out of Clement XIII, they managed to do from Clement XIV who dissolved the Society of Jesus in 1773. France responded by returning to the Papacy the recently occupied papal territories.

## 22. Pius VI and Revolutionary France

(a) The outbreak of the French Revolution in 1789 unleashed a very destructive force not only against anything that smelled of royalty and the aristocracy but also of anything Catholic. It was not only the French royals that lost their crowns, but also other European Crowns became eventually replaced in the name of liberty, equality and brotherhood, a movement extremely soaked in blood. The Catholic Church in France and wherever the French army occupied, especially the Papal States and the person of Pius VI, were special targets for the revolutionaries. It was not only a matter of replacing a Christian culture with the confused and conflicting brands of values proposed by the Enlightenment, but of creating a new world order which was imposed by violent and autocratic methods that were much worse than the methods which had been replaced. The ancient Catholic Church in France was suppressed, all Church and papal property in France was confiscated, and to add insult to injury, an effigy of Pius VI was burnt in front of the Palais Royal. The Pope did not react officially even when the Civil Constitution of the Clergy was enacted in July 1790. The document reorganized the entire French Catholic Church and made the clergy the employees of the State. But when the French regime demanded that the clergy take an oath of loyalty to it, Pius VI reacted by denouncing the Constitution as schismatic, suspending all the priests and bishops who took the oath, declared the ordination of the new State-appointed bishops as harmful to the universal Church and the Church in France, and condemned the 1789 Declaration of the Rights of Man. France retaliated by annexing the papal enclaves of Avignon and Venaissin, severing diplomatic relations with the Holy See, and declaring the French Church to be completely independent of Rome. Next, Pius VI threw his weight behind the First Coalition[9] whose aim was to contain the expansion of France and its revolutionary ideas.

(b) A brilliant, very angry and vindictive General Napoleon Bonaparte occupied Milan in 1796 and insisted that Pius VI withdraw his condemnation of the French Civil Constitution and the French Revolution. When the Pope refused to do so, Napoleon invaded the Papal States and forced the humiliating Truce of Bologna in 1796. But he refused to dethrone the Pope, despite the wishes of the atheistic members of the French Directory. Next came the Peace of Tolentino in 1797, the occupation of the Papal States, the deposition of the Pope as head of the Papal

---

[9] The membership of the First Coalition was comprised eventually of Austria, Prussia, Britain, the German States, Spain, Sardinia, Portugal, Naples and Sicily, and the Dutch Republic.

States, the declaration of the Roman Republic, and the imprisonment of the Pope. When he died, many anti-Catholics throughout
Europe thought that the demise of the Holy See had finally arrived. However, Pius VI had left instructions which outlined a
conclave under emergency conditions. Since Rome was occupied
by French troops, thirty-four of the forty-five Cardinal-Electors
met in conclave in Venice under the protection of Austria on 1$^{st}$
December 1799. There was a Sede Vacante for over six months
before a new Pope was elected. Of the four French Cardinal-
Electors, only the exiled Cardinal Jean-Siffrein Maury took part
in the conclave which elected Pius VII.

---

### 23. The Occupation of the Papal States

---

(a) Pius VI's pontificate was marked with grave tensions between
Rome and Paris due to the inimical new First French Republic.
Thus, he witnessed the Church's suppression, endured the con-
fiscation of papal and other Church possessions, and a violent
Church persecution throughout France. Soon, he erroneously
threw in his lot with the First Coalition against France.

Napoleon invaded the Italian peninsula in 1796, occupied a
large part of papal territory, and ignored the orders of the atheistic
French Directory by not marching against Rome lest he alienated Italian and French Catholic sympathies. The Pope sued for
peace. The Treaty of Tolentino of 1797 ceded a major part of the
Papal States to the new Cisalpine Republic. Much of the Church
property in northern Italy continued to fall into French hands.
As the Russian army pushed down on the French from northern
Italy and a riot in Rome at the end of December 1797 led to the
murder of General Duphot of the French embassy, the pretext to

invade Rome was finally found! General Berthier occupied Rome
with no opposition in mid-February 1798, declared a Roman
Republic, and demanded of the Pope to renounce his temporal
powers. After Pius VI refused to comply with the French demands,
he was arrested and taken prisoner, being moved from one place
to another, always toward France. When France declared war
against Grand Duke Ferdinand III of Tuscany, the Pope was
harried away until he was housed in Valence where he died at
the end of August 1799.

   (b) Just as the end of Pius VI's pontificate was pestered with
the rising star of Napoleon, Pius VII had to deal with him for the
first fifteen years of his pontificate.[10] By the time that Pius VII
was elected Pope, Napoleon had already managed a coup d'etat
and replaced the Directory with the Consulate, becoming the
First of three Consuls for France. Pius VII and the First Consul
were in constant conflict. Napoleon badgered and then demanded
from the Pope all kinds of rights and concessions and the Pope,
in turn, tried to temper the effects of these by making his own
demands for the Papacy. Thus, Pius VII asked for the restoration of the Papal States and his return to Rome, the liberty of
thirteen Black Cardinals[11] and the release or return to France of
many imprisoned or exiled religious or members of the hierarchy.
Pius VII was able to enter Rome in July 1800, and thereupon he
insisted upon the neutrality of the Papal States. Next came the
famous 1801 Concordat between Rome and Paris.[12] Napoleon
entered into the Concordat for sheer political reasons. It would

---

[10] See E.E.Y. Hales, *The Emperor and the Pope: The Story of Napoleon and Pius VII*,
NY: Octagon Books (1978); M.M. O'Dwyer, *The Papacy in the Age of Napoleon
and the Restoration: Pius VII, 1800-1823*, Lanham, MD: UPA (1985).

[11] These were the thirteen Cardinals who snubbed the marriage of Napoleon to
Marie Louise, believing that his first marriage was still valid.

[12] See n. 38.

govern the relations between France and Rome for the next one hundred years.

(c) Napoleon declared himself Emperor in 1804. More tension ensued when the Pope refused to annul the marriage between Napoleon's brother, Jerome Bonaparte, and Elizabeth Patterson in 1805. Napoleon, through diplomatic pressure brought about the dissolution of the one thousand eight year-old Holy Roman Empire in 1806. He also assumed control of southern Italy by making his older brother Joseph King of the Two Sicilies in 1806 and afterward King of Spain in 1808. The Pope was angered and refused to acknowledge Joseph's royal title. When the Pope also refused to subsidize France's military conflict with Britain, Napoleon had Rome once again occupied by French soldiers and confiscated more papal territory in Italy. Then, in May 1809, Napoleon declared the Papal States as part of the French Empire. He was excommunicated by the Pope and, in retaliation, the Pope was taken prisoner to France. He would remain there until he was freed by the Allied forces in May 1814. The Pope's return to Rome was triumphant.

After Napoleon was finally exiled to St. Helena Island, the Pope, to his great credit, wrote to the British government, asking for a better treatment of the former emperor. Moreover, in an utmost Christian spirit, the Pope also offered asylum to the Bonaparte family members. Meanwhile, the Congress of Vienna, among many of its decisions, restored the Papal States to Pius VII.

Despite the fact that Pius VII welcomed the restoration of the French Bourbons, Louis XVIII resisted any resumption of papal jurisdiction in France. The Pope unsuccessfully tried to modify the 1801 Concordat. Nevertheless, he was able to establish another thirty new dioceses in France in 1822.

# CHAPTER SIX

# Rome and Vienna

## 24. Popes and Emperor Charles VI

(a) Innocent XII's relations with Vienna became so strained due to the conceited imperial ambassador, Count Martinitz, that he advised Charles II of Spain to designate French Duke Philip of Anjou as his testamentary successor. This led to the War of the Spanish Succession.[1]

Cardinal Giovanni Francesco Albani was still a priest when elected as Pope Clement XI in November 1700, having refused his election for three days. The forty-six day conclave had been beset with secular political intrigues, including a French veto to Cardinal Galeazzo Mariscotti. Clement XI was consecrated Bishop of Rome on 30th November 1700. His timid character and inability to decide unless he was pushed had adverse effects for the Holy See. These elements manifested themselves before his papal election and in subsequent ambiguous dealings with European Crowns. He was confronted with an international crisis at the beginning of his pontificate due to the death of Charles II of Spain. The French Cardinals had promoted Albani because he had indicated a positive opinion on the rights of Philip of Bourbon to become the next King of Spain.

---

[1] See n. 41.

The War of the Spanish Succession put Clement XI in a very precarious position for he found himself in the middle of a very long war among mostly Catholic Crowns. He held a hazy neutrality, failed to broker a peace treaty, became openly involved against Austria when the imperial army occupied much of northern Italy and threatened Rome itself, and was bullied to name Archduke Charles of Austria as King of Spain[2] in 1709 despite his personal preference for the already crowned Philip V. He ended up displeasing all sides, lost much papal prestige, was shunned from taking part in the ensuring peace treaties, saw the dismissal of the papal feudal rights in southern Italy and Sicily, and Austria replaced the supremacy of Spain in Italy.

(b) Archduke Charles succeeded his brother Joseph I as Emperor Charles VI in 1711. He had a serious gripe to settle with the Holy See and made sure the price was paid by a number of succeeding Popes during his long imperial reign of twenty-nine years. His plan began to unfold with the Treaty of Utrecht in 1713, which ended the War of the Spanish Succession. The Holy See came out a great loser, with much papal territory ceded to Austria.

The conclave to elect Clement XI's successor was stormy. It lasted five long weeks. Cardinal Mihály Frigyes Althan of Vác presented Austria's veto against Cardinal Fabrizio Paolucci, while Spain vetoed Cardinal Francesco Pignatelli. Finally, Cardinal Michelangelo Conti was unanimously elected Pope in May 1721 and took the name Innocent XIII. His ancestors had already

---

[2]  Portugal, England, Scotland, Ireland and the majority of the Crowns within the Holy Roman Empire endorsed Charles's claim to the Spanish throne. He landed in Spain in 1706 and stayed there for the next five years, only able to exercise his lordship over Catalonia. He abandoned Spain and returned to Austria to succeed his brother Emperor Joseph I in 1711.

provided the Church with three Popes.[3] The new Pope was a seasoned diplomat, but of weak physical constitution.[4] Unfortunately his diplomatic skills deserted him once he became Pope. His pronounced aversion toward the Jesuits was welcomed in Vienna, Paris, Madrid, Naples, and Lisbon, among other European capitals. In order to gain support for Venice and the Knights of Malta in their war with the Turks, he began to lavishly bestow papal favors on secular rulers. He invested Charles VI with the Kingdom of the Two Sicilies as a result of the Treaty of Utrecht, thereby prolonging foreign presence on Italian soil. Charles VI turned around and invested the Spanish Prince Don Carlos, the future Charles III of Spain, with Parma and Piacenza, despite the Pope's vigorous protests that these were papal fiefdoms. The Pope was also unsuccessful in procuring the withdrawal of the imperial forces from occupied Comacchio, and to prevent the emperor from claiming supreme authority over the Church in Sicily despite the fact that Clement XI had already abolished the Sicilian monarchy in 1715. Later Charles VI, to ensure his legitimate claim to Sicily, extracted a Papal Bull in 1728 from Benedict XIII, which, without recognizing the monarchy in Sicily, acknowledged the emperor as having effective control over the Church there.

The effectiveness of the Papacy with European powers continued to decline under Clement XII. As overlord of Parma and Piacenza, he stood by helpless as Charles VI asserted complete dominion over the two cities in the name of Don Carlos. More humiliations followed. The Pope switched allegiances rapidly during the War of the Polish Succession[5] and ended up being forced

---

[3] The three Popes were Innocent III (1198-1216), in whose memory the new Pope chose his papal name; Gregory IX (1227-1241); and Alexander IV (1254-1261).

[4] Cardinal Conti had resigned as Bishop of Viterbo (1712-1719) due to health reasons.

[5] See n. 43.

to acquiesce to the provisions of the treaties of Vienna of 1735 and
1738. When the Romans rebelled against the recruitment of Ital-
ians by the imperial army, Vienna and Naples severed diplomatic
relations with Rome in 1736. The Pope had to make substantial
concessions to Madrid and formally invest Don Carlos with the
Kingdom of the Two Sicilies in 1737.

## 25. Crisis in Vienna

Both Clement XII and Charles VI died in 1740. The issue of their
successors proved to be troublesome. Charles VI had left no male
heir and despite the Pragmatic Sanction of 1713,[6] the succession
was not smooth. On the other hand, the conclave to elect a new
Pope lasted six months. The Cardinals were divided. Cardinal
Troiano Acquaviva d'Aragona posted Spain's veto against Cardinal Pier Marcelino Corradini. Cardinal Lorenzo Lambertini, to
everyone's surprise, was elected Pope as a compromise candidate.
He took the name of Benedict XIV. He was a realist. He signed
a number of concordats, making substantial concessions to Sardinia and Naples in 1741, to Spain in 1753, and to Francis I of
Austria in 1757.

The death of Charles VI of Austria was followed by the
War of the Austrian Succession, a war which dragged on until
1748. Benedict XIV greatly displeased the new Austrian ruler,
Maria Theresa, for taking two months to recognize her heredi-
tary rights. He further alienated her when he recognized Prince
Charles Albert of Bavaria as the new Holy Roman Emperor in

---

[6]   See n. 39 (a).

1742. Vienna responded by seizing Church property and invading the Papal States.

Shortly after the imperial coronation of Charles Albert, his territories were overrun by the Austrian army, which also occupied Bavaria. The emperor fled to Frankfurt, formed an alliance with Frederick II of Prussia, fought back Maria Theresa in a series of battles during 1743 and 1744, and regained Bavaria. Soon after his death in January 1745, his son, Maximilian III of Bavaria, sued for peace with Austria. Maria Theresa secured the election of her husband as Holy Roman Emperor Francis I the following September and made him co-regent of her hereditary Hapsburg domains. The Pope had learned his lesson well and had been humiliated enough by Austria. Thus, he stayed neutral during the recent imperial election.

---

## 26. Popes and Emperor Joseph II

---

(a) The seasoned diplomat Clement XIII had to deal with Joseph II of Austria. The latter had created his personal version of things Catholic for his subjects and imposed Febronianism,[7] limiting papal power to what he perceived to be purely spiritual. Rome was alarmed. The Pope denounced Febronianism in 1764 and requested the bishops within the Empire to reject the movement. Their response was very slow and almost apathetic. The emperor, meanwhile, like other Catholic Crowns in Europe, kept pushing the Pope to suppress the Jesuits. In fact, this issue dominated the conclave that followed the death of Clement XIII in 1769. Cardinal Lorenzo Ganganelli was finally elected as Clement XIV with

---

[7] See n. 9.

the proviso that he would suppress the Society of Jesus. After a four year delay, he suppressed the Society. Yet, he was ineffectual in preventing the first partition of Poland by Austria, Prussia and Russia in 1772.

Joseph II was determined to establish the total subjugation of the Catholic Church in Austria to the Crown. His Edict of Toleration of October 1781 suppressed some religious communities and transferred those monasteries that were under papal jurisdiction to that of local bishops. These bishops, in turn, supported these decisions without realizing that they were now subject to the whims of the Imperial Crown. The Pope made a futile journey to Vienna in 1782 to discuss these matters with the Emperor. Next, when the Pope sought to erect a Nunciature in Munich in 1786, the German bishops bluntly told him that the German Catholic Church was run by its bishops and did not need any papal involvement.

(b) Pius VII[8] was a relative of Pius VI. He seemed accommodating in that, once Napoleon declared the new Cisalpine Republic, he cautioned restraint and submission to the French program. His famous Christmas homily of 1797 asserted that there was no contradiction between a democratic government and being a good Catholic since equality among people comes from Christ.[9]

The Cardinal-Electors met in Venice under the protection of Francis II of Austria to elect the successor to Pius VI. Though the emperor posted his vote against two *papabili*, his own candidate, Cardinal Alessandro Mattei, could not secure enough electoral

---

8  See R. Anderson, *Pope Pius VII*, TAN Books & Publishers, Inc. (2001); P. Levillain (ed.), "Pius VII," op. cit.; *ODCC*, "Pius VII," op. cit.; Kelly, "Pius VII," op. cit.

9  See T. Bokenkotter, *Church and Revolution: Catholics in the Struggle for Democracy and Social Justice*, NY: Doubleday (1998).

votes. The blocking of the imperial candidate speaks a lot about the courage of the voting Cardinals. The conclave lasted more than three months and finally Cardinal Chiaramonti emerged as Pius VII in March 1800. He was crowned Pope in Venice, wearing a papier-mâché papal tiara because the French had seized the original one. The Austrians brought him by ship to Pesaro and from there he reached Rome by land.

One of his first acts as Pius VII was to appoint Ercole Consalvi, not yet in major holy orders, as his Secretary of State. After Consalvi was created a Cardinal, he continued to faithfully serve the Pope even when Napoleon forced him out of office as Secretary of State. After the Pope was freed from his captivity, Consalvi was restored to the office and he discharged it with great diplomacy, particularly at the Congress of Vienna, which restored the Papal States to the Pope. Only a small area of the Papal States remained under Austria.

Europe retreated toward conservatism after the Congress of Vienna and began the era of Restoration under the vigilant eye of Prince Klemens von Metternich, the Austrian chancellor and probably the most capable diplomat during this era. The Holy Alliance that had been formed against Napoleon now had to make peace with France and restore order and stability to Continental Europe. The reform in Austria initiated by Joseph II ended. However, most of the religious changes imposed by Josephism remained in the Austrian Church. The Austrian government continued to control all religious activities. The State embarked on a meticulous censorship program of any kind of anti-clerical literature, though many government bureaucrats wanted to curtail further the Church's temporal power. They eventually found their leader in Metternich who veiled his policy of subordinating the Church to the State through conservatism. Metternich understood very well the conservatism of his Hapsburg sovereign who wanted a religious revival after the violent anti-clericalism of the French Revolution and the Napoleonic Wars. Both Rome and Vienna feared modernization because they determined it led to revolutions. Metternich, like all other conservative European governments, aimed at preventing revolution, but he and the emperor were not comfortable with the Holy Alliance which had been formed at the promptings of Czar Alexander I of Russia in 1815. It aimed at instilling Christian principles into political life. Metternich felt that he had to resist the call from some Catholic quarters to roll back Josephism. This resistance, in turn, continued to deepen the strains between Vienna and Rome. A great source of the tension was due to the easy way a Protestant could marry a Catholic, called a mixed marriage. It became more intense as Catholic clergy began to refuse to perform such marriages. Though Austria allowed the Jesuits to return in 1820, the Society was subjected to intense State oversight.

# CHAPTER SEVEN

# Rome and Madrid

## 27. Rome and the Spanish Hapsburgs

(a) As was the case with Benedict XIII, Clement XII's foreign policy saw further decline in international papal prestige. The diplomatic relations between Madrid and Rome were temporarily broken off in 1736, but were restored within two years, with the Pope being forced to make substantial concessions to the Spanish Crown. Clement XII saw the European Catholic States increasingly affirming their secular superiority over the Church in their respective domains, with Spain being no exception. On the other hand, the 1753 Concordat between Benedict XIV and Ferdinand VI of Spain proved damaging to inner Church governance. There was too much government control. The Spanish Padronado[1] became supreme in Spain and in its vast territories.

Clement XIII was embroiled in the resolve of the European Catholic powers to have the Jesuits suppressed. Despite his pleas with the Spanish Crown, the Jesuits were expelled from all Bourbon Spanish domains during 1767. The Pope had no intention to suppress the Jesuits and called a special consistory in Rome for

---

[1] The Spanish Padronado was similar to the Portuguese Padroado. See n. 17.

3rd February 1769, just to die the day before its assembly. The conclave that followed, dominated by the Bourbons' demands to elect a Pope who would suppress the Jesuits, was a very stormy three month ordeal. For the first time in centuries, all the Cardinals, fifty-seven in total, participated and voted. The conclave concluded with the election of Cardinal Lorenzo Ganganelli as Clement XIV. The Bourbons soon reminded him of the Jesuits' fate. He promised quick action, but in fact did nothing for the next four years except hoping for a compromise that entailed a complete reorganization of the Society and a temporary suspension of its recruitment program. The Pope was finally prevailed upon when the Bourbons threatened a complete break with Rome and Empress Maria Theresa, up till then pro-Jesuit, declared her neutrality in the matter. The Brief of Suppression, entitled *Dominus ac Redemptor noster*, was prepared amid active consultation with the Spanish embassy and was handed to the Jesuit leadership on 16th August 1773. The secular rulers hailed the act as a triumph for the Enlightenment. The only two sovereigns who did not enforce the suppression were the Russian Orthodox Catherine the Great and the Protestant Frederick the Great of Prussia. The suppression of the Society, in fact, resulted in a severe damage to the Catholic school system and missionary work. This pontificate took papal prestige to its lowest level in centuries. Yet, more humiliations were in store for his immediate successors.

Cardinal Giovanni Angelo Braschi was elected as Pius VI in February 1775 after a 134-day conclave. He made the pro and anti Jesuits factions in the conclave think that he was on their respective side. His long pontificate would delve the Holy See further down in its prestige. He was devastatingly humiliated in his old age. He witnessed the rapid rising of secularism and atheism, of the intransigence of Catholic monarchs to control the Church within their respective domains, and the French Revolution with its violent anti-clericalism program.

(b) The Bourbons in Naples refused feudal homage to the Holy See and Ferdinand IV insisted on his right to present his choice of bishops. Pius VI simply withheld the canonical installation of every one of such bishops. Many dioceses remained without a Chief Shepherd. However, the Pope, pushed by the Bourbon Crowns in Europe, half-heartedly tried to exert pressure on Catherine of Russia and Frederick of Prussia to suppress the Jesuits in their domains. Empress Catherine, in fact, allowed the Jesuits to establish a novitiate in her empire in 1780. Subsequently, the Pope granted his secret approval.

(c) Joseph Bonaparte was imposed as King of Spain in 1808, replacing the Spanish Bourbons. During his brief reign, ending with his abdication in 1813, the Spanish Inquisition[2] was abolished, and Central and South American Spanish colonies began their series of wars for independence.

Ferdinand VII regained his Spanish throne after Joseph's abdication. He immediately allowed the recently restored Jesuits to become active again in Spain. However, the Spanish liberals soon identified them with repression and absolutism. The king also restored the Spanish Inquisition in 1814, which remained a branch of the Spanish government. It would be definitively abolished in 1834 by the regent Queen Maria Christina, the king's fourth wife.

A very serious rebellion broke out in Spain in 1820 and the king became a pawn. Rome was very concerned because of

---

[2]  See R. Sabatini, *Torquemada and the Spanish Inquisition: A History*, Kessinger Publishing (2003); E. Peters, *Inquisition, Dissent, Heterodoxy and the Medieval Inquisitional Office*, UCP (1989); A. Borromeo (ed.), *L'Inquisizione*, Città del Vaticano: BAV (2003); Spiteri, *At Your Fingertips* III, n. 13.

its anti-clerical tone. Jesuits were hunted down and prosecuted, with twenty-five of them being executed in 1822. Church courts were outlawed, many monasteries were suppressed, and financial contributions to Rome were prohibited. Moreover, an ambassador to Rome, who was renowned for advocating the abolition of the Papacy, was named. Pius VII refused to acknowledge the ambassador and broke off diplomatic relations with Madrid in 1823. Ferdinand VII's power, with the help of foreign powers, was restored later in 1823. However, the Jesuits would experience expulsions and re-establishment in Spain for the rest of the nineteenth century.

## 28. Latin America Revolts Against Madrid

Pius VII had to deal with revolutionary movements which took place in the New World where the majority of the inhabitants were Catholic and subject to Spain. The situation was very complicated by the fact that the local Catholic hierarchy was identified with the oppressive establishment, though some Catholic priests, as for example in Mexico, led some rebellions. Thus, the rebelling parties did not only fight against the representatives of Spain but were also very anti-Church. The Pope, beleaguered by Napoleon and his own problems in the Papal States and with European sovereigns who were attempting to wrestle away from the Church her members and the patrimony of local churches, was also responsible to ensure that the Catholic Faith was not extinguished in the New World. News traveled slowly at this time, but when they reached the papal ear, Pius VII had good reason to be gravely concerned, though he was essentially powerless to intervene in an effective manner.

Haiti's slaves began their revolt against France in 1791 and became independent at the beginning of 1804. The event had a domino effect through Central and South America whose peoples rose against Spain. Bolivia declared its independence in 1809, but would not gain it until 1825. Paraguay became independent in 1811. Venezuela revolted and declared its first independence in 1811, becoming definitively independent of Spain in 1821. Colombia became independent in 1820. The first revolt in Ecuador broke out in 1809 and it became independent in 1822. Argentina revolted in 1810 and declared its independence in 1816, though this did not become a fact until 1818. Uruguay revolted in 1811 and became fully independent in 1825. Chile revolted in 1810, declared its independence in 1818 and Spain recognized it until 1840. Peru rebelled in 1812 and declared its independence in 1821. Finally, Mexico began its revolt in 1810 and won its independence in 1821, along with Guatemala, El Salvador, Honduras, Costa Rica, and Nicaragua.

# CHAPTER EIGHT

# Rome and Lisbon

## 29. Rome Gives into Lisbon's Demands

(a) Innocent X, as his successor Alexander VII will do, sided with Spain against Portugal when the latter declared its independence from Spain in 1640. It re-established its autonomous monarchy with the House of Braganza providing the rulers. The Pope also refused to approve the appointment of all new bishops which the new Portuguese King, João IV, had nominated. It eventually resulted in Portugal having only one diocese ruled by a bishop.

Cardinal Giulio Rospigliosi was elected as Clement IX in 1667. He had worked very closely with Urban VIII and was eventually named Papal Nuncio to Spain. He fell out of favor during the pontificate of Innocent X, though he remained Papal Nuncio to Spain. He was back in favor with Alexander VII, who named him Cardinal and Secretary of State in 1657. Rospigliosi was elected his successor after an eighteen-day conclave. He made peace with Portugal and reorganized the Portuguese hierarchy.

Innocent XIII had been nuncio in Portugal from 1698 to 1709. It was during his time in Portugal that the future Pope developed a sustaining aversion towards the Jesuits. He succeeded Clement XI in May 1721.

Though Clement XI and João V had agreed back in 1716 that the new Lisbon Patriarch should be made a Cardinal at the next consistory, the new Patriarch, Tomás de Almeida, had to wait until 1737 to become one. In the meantime, Benedict XIII, in an uncharacteristic move, crossed swords with João V in resisting the king's demand to propose Cardinalatial candidates, though other Catholic Crowns enjoyed this privilege. But José I, a weak ruler, managed to procure from Benedict XIV the right of Padroado. It was a huge mistake! The real power behind the throne at the time was the Marquis Pombal who, through his king, might as well have run the Catholic Church in Portugal and its vast domains. He assumed charge not only of the dreaded Portuguese Inquisition which functioned as an arm of the secular State but also of the appointment to major Church offices. Meanwhile, the Portuguese Cardinals Domenico Silvio and Alberico Archinto urged Benedict XIV to initiate a thorough reform of the Jesuits. The Pope finally capitulated and named Cardinal Francisco de Saldanha de Gama to investigate them. Subsequently, José I, following the advice of Pombal, deported the Jesuits from Portugal in 1758 and had them expelled from all the Portuguese territories the following year. They were all taken to the papal city of Civitavecchia. Then Pombal, in 1760, expelled the Papal Nuncio from Portugal, recalled the ambassador to the Holy See, and gave his nod to a smear campaign against the Jesuits, who were depicted as setting up a virtual kingdom in South America as subversive tyrants to the Indios. Having the Jesuits out of the picture, Pombal then intensified his meddling in Church affairs and imposed the Enlightenment philosophy on seminaries and institutions of higher education to the detriment of Catholic Church teachings.

Lisbon interfered, along with Spain and France, during the 1774-1775 papal conclave which elected Cardinal Giovanni

Carlo Boschi as Pius VI. The Cardinal was elected after these three countries dropped their veto against him. Subsequently, once Maria II ascended the Portuguese throne in 1777, Pombal was dismissed from office and relations warmed up between the Holy See and Lisbon. They were forged with a concordat in 1778. However, anti-clericalism remained a strong force in Portuguese society. Some forty years later, in 1821, the Portuguese Inquisition was abolished, religious orders were banned, and the Church lost much of its property once again.

(b) Portugal had declared its complete autonomy from Spain in 1640. The territory of the archdiocese of Lisbon expanded as the country grew in political importance and colonial possessions. Clement XI rewarded the Portuguese Crown in 1708 by raising the Royal Chapel to a Collegiate rank in recognition of the assistance the Crown gave against the Turks. Later, in 1716, João V requested the same Pope to bestow upon it the rank of a Patriarchal Basilica. Thus, the archdiocese of Lisbon was divided into two parts, Oriental and Occidental Lisbon. The old archdiocese became Oriental Lisbon and the new Occidental archdiocese became Lisbon's Titular Patriarchate. The division brought some confusion and so, in December 1740, Benedict XIV joined both metropolitan Sees into one archdiocese and the seat of the Patriarchate.

(c) Dom Pedro of Beira, son of João VI of Portugal, officially declared the independence of Brazil from Portugal in 1822 and proclaimed himself as Emperor Pedro I. When João VI died in 1826, he left behind two sons: Emperor Pedro I and Prince Miguel, who was exiled in Austria. The father had failed to indicate who of the two should succeed him. Portugal ended up with a succession crisis. Pedro I ruled Portugal for a few months and then abdicated the throne to his nine year-old daughter, Infanta

Isabel Maria, offering the Regency of Portugal to his brother Miguel with the proviso that the latter would uphold a constitutional monarchy and marry the Queen once she became of age. Miguel agreed. Subsequently, a coup d'etat took place and Miguel declared himself King. The Pope, Spain and the United States recognized him as the new ruler of Portugal. He was an absolute monarch and avidly waged war against liberals. Then Pedro I abdicated the Brazilian throne and led an army against his brother. After a civil war, which lasted three years, Miguel abdicated in 1834 and Maria II was restored to the throne. Miguel spent the rest of his life in exile and at a certain stage he was provided with housing in Rome by Gregory XVI.

Portugal and Brazil were separated in 1822. However, the Padroado system continued to exist in both countries. It meant that the sovereign of each respective country had a free hand in Church affairs.

---

## 30. The Portuguese Colonies in Asia

Portugal had many dealings with Rome due to the Catholic presence in Portugal's overseas territories not only in Brazil but also in other parts of the world. The Padroado created much tension between Rome and Lisbon and between missionaries sent by the Propaganda Fidei and those sent by Portugal.

(a) Alexander VI assigned the evangelization of countries in the East to the Portuguese in 1493. It was carried out as a Church-State joint venture. Portuguese missionaries arrived in India in 1500. Five years later, in 1505, a Portuguese fleet commanded by Lourenco de Almeida was driven by a storm to Colombo, Sri

Lanka. The presence of Catholicism arrived on the island by sheer accident! At the time, the island was comprised of a number of kingdoms. Julius II was informed of this event in 1507.

Portugal slowly became steadily involved in the island's politics. It sent Franciscan missionaries to convert the Sri Lankan royal families and their subjects. Other religious communities arrived in due time but, sadly, there was too much fighting amongst them. Conversions began at a slow pace. Over the years Catholics experienced repression and persecution, ultimately ending with banishment or martyrdom.

King Senarat Bandāra of Kandy signed a peace treaty with Portugal in 1617. Rajasimha succeed his father Bandāra in 1635. He managed to expel the Portuguese from the island with the assistance of Dutch Calvinists. The king and his subjects soon realized that they had simply changed masters. Kandy was highly resistant to Catholicism, though this was not the case with the Kingdoms of Kotte and Jaffna especially when they fell under direct Portuguese rule.

(b) The first recorded Portuguese presence in Siam, modern-day Thailand, was in 1544. The missionary Antonio de Paiva had met, instructed and baptized the Siamese King. The Portuguese Padroado went into effect. A very small number of missionaries followed him until the arrival of the Jesuits in 1607. The latter established their residence, erected a school, and immediately became involved in educating the natives.

The Sacred Congregation of Propaganda Fidei[1] was established in 1622 with the specific purpose of focusing on all Catholic missions and missionary activities. It provided its own Vicars for missionary areas. Thus, it was just a matter of a short

---

[1] Today it is known as the Congregation for the Evangelization of Peoples.

time for conflict to arise between the Vicars from Propaganda and the Padroado, which controlled much inner Church affairs that included the nomination of Bishops. When the first French missionaries arrived in Siam in 1662, they were welcomed by ten Portuguese and one Spanish priest. With the French arrival, the Portuguese influence in Siam diminished rapidly.

# CHAPTER NINE

# Rome and London

## 31. Catholics Persecuted

The persecution of Catholics in England did not stop with the death of Elizabeth I in 1603. She was succeeded by James VI, son of Mary Queen of Scots.[1] He was acknowledged as James I of England and James VI of Scotland, and the two kingdoms were distinctly and separately ruled by the same King. Persecution of Catholics in England intensified due to the foolish and ill-fated Gunpowder Plot, a conspiracy planned by a small group of Catholic schemers, largely led by Guy Fawkes. It aimed at blowing up both King and Parliament. The plot was discovered on 5th November 1605. Yet, the king did tolerate some Catholics at his court, such as George Calvert, to whom he gave the title Baron Baltimore, and, of course, the Duke of Norfolk, head of the Howard family.[2]

Catholicism, especially among the upper classes and due to political reasons, saw a minor revival under Charles I,[3] who had

---

[1] See A. Fraser, *Mary Queen of Scots*, London: Orion Books, 2nd printing (2003); Spiteri, *At Your Fingertips* III, n. 48 (d) (iii).

[2] See B. Coward, *The Stuart Age*, London: Longman (1994).

[3] See R. Dutton, *English Court Life: From Henry VII to George II*, London: B.T. Batsford (1963); R. Cust, *Charles I: A Political Life*, London: Longman (2005).

married the Catholic Henrietta Maria of France. At the time, the rise of Puritanism and Calvinism in England displayed elements of being anti-monarchical and anti-aristocratic. To counteract this trend, the King and some of the nobility adopted "High Church" Anglicanism which was less anti-Catholic in character. The king also, though not always, refused to enforce anti-Catholic laws and allowed a visible increase in the number of Catholic clergy who even gained some converts.

One of the many elements that led to the English Civil War was the tensions between a Puritan Parliament and a court with "Papist" elements. Charles I received the support of most of the English Catholics, along with the Anglicans, during the said war. Accordingly, the victory of the Parliamentarians meant a strongly Protestant, anti-Catholic and anti-Anglican regime under Oliver Cromwell. Irish Catholics were also very aggressively and extraordinarily persecuted.[4]

When the English monarchy was restored under Charles II in 1660,[5] the royal court witnessed the return of Catholic influence. The king had Catholic tendencies, but he was pragmatic. He recognized that the majority of his English subjects were strongly anti-Catholic. Thus, he agreed to the enactment of such laws as the Test Act which required any appointee to any public office to officially deny Catholic beliefs. But he married the Portuguese Catholic Catherine of Braganza in 1662 and held tacit tolerance of Catholics.

---

[4] See M. Cronin, op. cit.; M. McAuliffe *et al*, op. cit.
[5] See A. Fraser, *King Charles II*, London: Weidenfeld and Nicolson (1979); T. Harris, *Restoration: Charles II and His Kingdoms, 1660-1685*, London: Allen Lane (2005).

## 32. Rome and James II

(a) James, Duke of York,[6] younger brother and heir to Charles II, became a Catholic some time in 1668-1669. When Titus Oates, in 1678, alleged a totally imaginary "Popish Plot" to assassinate Charles II and replace him with James, the king allowed a wave of parliamentary and public hysteria that led to anti-Catholic purges and another sectarian persecution. But, the attempt by the Whig element in Parliament failed to exclude James as heir to the throne. He became King James II in 1685 and was the first Catholic monarch since Mary I.

After James II became king, Blessed Innocent XI sent Ferdinando d'Adda as Papal Nuncio to England, the first ever in more than one hundred years. But the Pope was so displeased with James II's reckless rule that he did not assist him when the Protestant William III, Holland's Stadtholder and James II's son-in-law and nephew, invaded England to claim its throne in 1688. It is also doubtful whether James II was genuinely interested in restoring Catholicism.

(b) Despite the fact that the Pope did not intervene on behalf of James II, there were adverse repercussions for English Catholics under the new Protestant sovereigns, who assumed the names of William III and Mary II.[7] All Catholic dioceses were abolished. English Catholics had to be content with four Apostolic Vicariates throughout England until the re-establishment

---

[6] See L. Glassey, (ed.), *The Reigns of Charles II and James VII and II*, Basingstoke: Macmillan (1997); J. Callow, *The Making of King James II: The Formative Years of a King*, Gloucestershire: Sutton Publishing, Ltd. (2000).

[7] See S. Pincus, *England's Glorious Revolution: A Brief History with Documents*, NY: Palgrave Macmillan (2006); idem., *1688: The First Modern Revolution*, New Haven: YUP (2009); S. Pincus and P. Lake (eds.), *The Politics of the Public Sphere in Early Modern England*, Manchester: MUP (2007).

of the English Catholic hierarchy in 1850. Catholic persecution was not as violent as in the past, but Catholics became isolated non-entities in English society, except for a handful of aristocrats at court, particularly the noble Howard family,[8] whose influence was rather negligible at the time. Catholic recusants, that is those who openly refused to attend Anglican services, suffered a heavy special tax, could not send their children to study overseas, could not vote, could not occupy any prominent public or military or professional place in society, and they were greatly restricted in owning property and land inheritance. Moreover, Catholic priests could be imprisoned at any moment. It was a very subtle persecution.

As was the case with Clement XI, Innocent XIII gave an annual pension to the "Old" Pretender, James Stewart, the son of James II, and also promised financial assistance should the opportunity present itself to regain the English Crown. The maneuver put English and Scottish Catholics in a very delicate predicament and papal prestige suffered among them. There was a further downturn when the Pope offered refuge to the "Old" Pretender after the unsuccessful 1715 Scottish uprising.

(c) St. Anselm of Canterbury is a saint recognized by both Catholics and Anglicans. Thus, when Clement XI proclaimed him a Doctor of the Church in 1720, the news was welcomed in Protestant England. Thirty-two years later, in 1752, as a subtle sign that things between London and Rome were slightly improving, Britain adopted the calendar that had been established by Gregory

---

[8]   The ancient noble Howard family included its head, the Duke of Norfolk who was also the Premier Duke in the English peerage and, as Earl of Arundel, the Premier Earl. Other members of the Howard family were the Earls of Carlisle, Suffolk, Berkshire, and Effingham. The Howards supplied England with some Catholic martyrs and, ironically, with two Protestant Queens, Anne Boleyn and Catherine Howard, both wives of Henry VIII and both beheaded by him.

XIII in 1582. However, when the Catholic Relief Act was passed in 1778, allowing Catholics to own property, inherit land and join the army, hard-nosed Protestants turned into dreadful mobs and caused the Gordon Riots of 1780. They destroyed buildings in London owned by either Catholics or those associated with them. But, soon thereafter, Catholics began to see some concrete liberalization of anti-Catholic laws. Further reforms in British laws permitted the Catholic clergy to minister more openly and allowed the erection of permanent missions in the larger towns.

One Catholic who rose to rare prominence, despite very strong anti-Catholic feelings at the time, was the English essayist, critic, satirist, and one of the greatest poets of the Enlightenment, Alexander Pope. Another famous recusant was Anne Maria Fitzherbert who, in 1785, secretly married the Prince Regent George, Prince of Wales and the future George IV. He was her third husband. Though Pius VII acknowledged the validity of the marriage, it was considered null according to the Royal Marriage Act of 1772 for lacking the approval of the reigning king, George III, and the Privy Council.

Catholics in the English Colonies in America fell under the jurisdiction of the Vicar Apostolic of London. It was only after the Treaty of Paris in 1783 that, in 1789, Pius VI gave the recently established United States of America the former Jesuit John Carroll, a friend of Benjamin Franklin, as the first diocesan bishop. The relationship between Rome and the young United States is discussed in a subsequent chapter.

CHAPTER TEN

# Rome and Fragmented Italy

## 33. Rome and Italian Principalities

(a) Since Italy was comprised of many small independent States, Popes had to deal with them individually and, at times, collectively.[1] The strained papal relations with Venice under Urban VIII were completely thawed during the pontificate of Innocent X. He supplied assistance to the Venetians who at the time were fighting the Turks that were besieging the Venetian possession of Crete. In return, the grateful Venetians allowed the Pope to freely appoint new bishops to their vacant dioceses, thus relinquishing the Republic's right to make such nominations. However, he launched another papal armed attack on the ancient city of Castro that was under the control of the Farnese Duke of Parma, Ranuccio II. The city was totally razed to the ground in 1649. The Duke was forced to cede control of the territories around Castro back to the Pope, who then tried to use the land to settle accounts with the Duke's creditors. The Duchy of Parma and Piacenza continued to be ruled by the Farnese until 1731 when the last duke, Antonio Farnese, died without direct heirs. The succession would prove to be a papal headache.

---

[1] See E. Duffy, *Saints and Sinners: A History of the Popes*, YUP (1997).

Papal support for Venice continued under the successors of Innocent X. Alexander VII pledged papal assistance to Venice against the Turks on the condition that the Jesuits were able to return to Venetian territory from where they had been expelled in 1606. On the other hand, Clement IX failed to gain wide support in Europe for the Venetian war against the Turks and, after a twenty year long siege, Crete fell to its besiegers in October 1699.

(b) The Italian policy of Benedict XIII was not always successful. He assisted the Venetians and the Knights of Malta in their struggle against the Turks. He invested Emperor Charles VI with the Kingdom of Two Sicilies, thereby further entrenching Austrian presence on Italian soil. The Emperor, in turn, invested the Spanish Prince Don Carlos with Parma and Piacenza, ignoring the Pope's vigorous protests that these duchies were under papal suzerainty.

As was the case with the previous pontificate, Clement XII's foreign policy saw further decline. There was the failed and disavowed attempt to seize papal possession of the independent tiny Republic of San Marino; the War of the Polish Succession that was partially fought on Italian soil; the invasion of the Papal States by foreign armies; the Austrian rebuff of Papal claims to the Duchies of Parma and Piacenza; the extension of Austrian power in the Grand Duchy of Tuscany; and the complete dismissal of Papal feudal rights over the Kingdom of the Two Sicilies. Clement XII in the main was totally ignored and forced to accept decisions without being given a hearing in any Italian political matter. He was helpless in witnessing the shift of power in Italy, enacted by the Treaties of Vienna of 1735 and 1738. In May 1736, Spain and the Kingdom of the Two Sicilies broke off diplomatic relations with the Holy See. Within two years, he was forced to make substantial concessions to the Spanish Crown and unconditionally invest Don Carlos as the King of the Two Sicilies in 1738 so as to restore diplomatic relations with both kingdoms. Conversely, Benedict XIV resolved most of the problems between the Holy See and the Kingdoms of Naples and of Sardinia. The Pope was willing to make many concessions, thus forfeiting temporal claims but maintaining the substance of spiritual supremacy. His willingness to concede the right of patronage in Naples aimed at gaining more moral influence of the Papacy. He mediated and established a tribunal in Naples for ecclesiastical cases. The tribunal consisted of an equal number of clergy and laity, presided over by a cleric. All parties were appeased with the solution. He bestowed the title "Vicar of the Holy See" on the King of Sardinia. He allowed him to nominate clerics for all Church benefices within the kingdom and to receive the income of pontifical fiefs through a concordat. But Venice was angered when the Pope decided to suppress the Patriarchate of Aquileia and then divide it into two archdioceses, one under Austria and the other under Venice. The latter claimed to have received an unfair deal and retaliated by temporarily severing all ties with Rome in 1751.

Clement XIII was not only chagrined by the way the Bourbons in Italy treated the Jesuits, but also by the question of investiture in Parma. The latter occasioned a diplomatic rift between Austria and the Holy See. He also had to counteract the spreading of Jansenism in Venice. On the other hand, his successor, Clement XIV, did give into political pressures and suppressed the Society of Jesus. In so doing, he lost a great defender of the Church against the encroaching secularism of the Enlightenment. He, too, had to deal with the issue of Parma and Piacenza, Spain's alleged claims over Benevento and Pontecorvo, and Naples' push to expand its territory adjoining the Papal States.

Pius VI was faced with Napoleon and with a variety of major problems with some Italian Principalities. Archduke Leopold of Tuscany tried to control wholly the Church in his domain and to impose Gallican and Enlightenment policies, along with Jansenism. Yet, the Pope did not immediately condemn the decrees of the heretical Synod of Pistoia in 1786 and move against the episcopal loyalty to them, but waited some eight years before he acted. In contrast, Joseph II of Austria did not hesitate to fill the vacant See of Milan. Pius VI vehemently protested and threatened him with excommunication. The situation was defused through a new concordat in 1784 in which the Pope gave the emperor the right to nominate the bishops of Milan and Mantua. Sardinia and Venice attempted to follow the emperor's policies. But the greatest challenge in Italy came from Naples, which passed sweeping anti-Church reforms that denied papal authority and affirmed the king's right to nominate anyone to a Church benefice. The Pope refused to accept any of the king's nominations and the kingdom ended up with more than thirty vacant dioceses in 1784, which doubled in number by 1798.

(c) Pius VII had to deal with the occupying armies of Napoleon all over Italy. After the restoration of the Papal States, Pius VII accepted the bitter fact that the Church that had been reshaped by Metternich, and whose policies also influenced a great part of Italy, was less influential than she was before the revolutionary period. Austria, which held a foothold in northern Italy, did not repudiate Josephism. Nonetheless, the Pope found the reactionary atmosphere in Europe to be rather satisfying since he, too, resisted further social changes. Yet, the Napoleonic social legislation was not repealed. Furthermore, Pius VII also had to deal with the emerging power of the secret societies of Freemasons and the Carbonari. The latter was born and bred in

Italy and was an Italian secret anti-clerical society with liberal and patriotic ideals that favored constitutional and representative governments in all of Italy, similar to the one in England. He issued two encyclicals in which they were condemned. His successor, Leo XII, was faced with the same secret societies and he, too, condemned them.

The July 1830 Revolution in France overthrew the Bourbon dynasty and the Duke of Orleans became King Louis Philippe, the citizen king. One of his first acts was to seize Ancona in 1831. This produced a frightening effect all over Italy, particularly on Gregory XVI. Austria was called upon a number of times to assist against the Italian republican-minded groups who had initiated a terrorist campaign. The French troops remained in Ancona until the departure of the Austrian troops from the Papal States in 1838. In the meantime, much anti-Catholic propaganda was circling in Italy, calling for the abolition of the Papal States. The Pope counteracted by condemning such ideas and the movements behind them and advocating basic totalitarianism throughout Italy, setting up roadblocks to any progressive movements and ignoring all popular rights.

Napoleon, by arbitrarily remapping Italy, laid the foundation for its future unity as one nation. Pius IX lived through it and, in opposing the annexation of Rome in 1870, declared himself to be the "Prisoner in the Vatican." Thus, a decision that was taken some seventy years earlier by a foreign power found its fruition. With the year of revolutions breaking out in 1848, Louis Philippe fled Paris, Metternich resigned as chancellor and fled Vienna, Italy revolted to throw off the Austrian yoke, and the liberal-minded Pius IX who had been sympathetic to establish a united Italy under his leadership, fled Rome.

# CHAPTER ELEVEN

# Rome and the United States of America

The presence of Catholics in the United States goes back to the beginning of the sixteenth century. However, these historic places did not form part of the original Thirteen Colonies which declared their independence from England and formed the United States of America. At the time, Catholics were very small in number in the new nation and underwent great discrimination, despite the fact that some Catholics had played a very prominent part in the establishment of the Republic.[1]

Two prominent Catholics, Daniel Carroll and Thomas Fitzsimmons, were members of the Continental Congress which met in Philadelphia to frame the United States Constitution in 1787. Finally, due to the ratification of the First Amendment to the American Constitution in 1791, which officially granted freedom of religion to all American citizens, the anti-Catholic laws which were in the statute books of the original thirteen States began to be repealed.

---

[1] Such persons were Count Casimir Pulaski, Tadeusz Kosciuszko, de Grasse, Count Jean-Baptiste Donatien de Vimeur de Rochambeau, Count Charles Hector d'Estaing, the Marquis de Lafayette.

---

## 34. The First American Bishop

---

(a) Pius VI approved the election of John Carroll as the first Catholic Bishop in the United States in November 1789.[2] He was the only bishop who was elected instead of being appointed by a Pope. After Carroll's episcopal ordination in Europe in 1790, he returned to the States and embarked on a very active episcopal ministry. Among his many accomplishments in the field of education was the founding of Georgetown University in 1791. He assembled the first diocesan Synod that same year. The Synod discussed the sacraments of baptism, confirmation, penance and reconciliation, and the anointing of the sick. Other topics were the celebration of the Liturgy, mixed marriages, fasting and abstinence, and Church finances. The synodical decrees were the first Church legislation in the young nation. Carroll also oversaw the construction of the first cathedral, located in Baltimore, in 1806.

(b) Pius VII seems to have been genuinely impressed with the young United States. When the latter demolished the Muslim Barbary Pirates along the southern Mediterranean coast, the Pope is reported to have said in 1804 that the United States did more for the cause of Christianity than the most powerful Christian nations had done for ages.[3]

---

[2]  See J.C. Tracy, *Documents of American Catholic History*, 2nd ed., Milwaukee: Bruce Publishing Co. (1956); T. Maynard, *The Story of American Catholicism*, 2 vols., NY: Macmillan Company (1960); N.C. Eberhardt, C.M., *A Survey of American Church History*, Vol. II, St. Louis: B. Herder Book Co. (1964); J. Hennesey, S.J., *American Catholics: A History of the Roman Catholic Community in the United States*, NY: OUP (1981); T.J. Jonas, *The Divided Mind: American Catholic Evangelists in the 1890s,* NY: Garland Press (1988); R. Middleton, *Colonial America*, Oxford: Blackwell Publishing (2003).

[3]  See J. Wheelan, *Jefferson's War: America's First War on Terror, 1801-1805*, Carroll & Graf (2004); J.E. London, *Victory in Tripoli: How America's War with the Barbary Pirates Established the U.S. Navy and Built a Nation,* John Wiley & Sons (2005).

Pius VII, recognizing the growing Catholic presence in the United States, elevated the Diocese of Baltimore to an Archdiocese in 1808 and established the dioceses of Boston, New York, Philadelphia and Bardstown. Then followed a provincial council in 1810 which asked that the nomination of bishops for the United States be made by the American hierarchy and not by European prelates. Pius VII also establish the dioceses of Charleston and Richmond in 1820 and of Cincinnati the following year. Furthermore, he reestablished the Society of Jesus in America in 1813.

The number of Catholics in the United States increased considerably with the Louisiana Purchase from France in 1803. The amount of territory gained was enormous, doubling the size of the country. It covered all of Arkansas, Iowa, Kansas, Missouri, Nebraska, Oklahoma, Wyoming, nearly all of South Dakota, Colorado east of the Continental Divide, Louisiana west of the Mississippi River, the section of Minnesota west of the Mississippi River, portions of Montana, northeastern New Mexico, and most of North Dakota.[4] However, although France had the privilege of nominating bishops within its domains, the privilege was not extended to the United States for, after all, its leadership was Protestant and there was a definite separation of Church and State in the nation. Next came the purchasing of Florida from Spain through the Adams-Onís Treaty of 1819, and then the incorporation of the northern territories of Mexico into the United States in 1847. The privilege of the Spanish Padronado was not extended to the United States government. Catholics formed the majority of all of these new territories since they had been evangelized by missionaries for a number of centuries. Then followed

---

[4] At the time of the purchase, Spain still claimed the Oklahoma Panhandle and southwestern portions of Kansas and Louisiana.

the admission of California to the Union in 1850. This, too, had a substantial Catholic population at the time.

## 35. American Prejudice

Catholicism had become the United States' largest single denomination by 1850 and has remained as such ever since. Irish Catholics constituted about one-third of all immigrants to the States during the middle years of the nineteenth century. At the time, the Church in the States was dominated by cultural French Catholics who did not welcome their Irish counterparts. Furthermore, although German American Catholics outnumbered Irish Catholics, the majority of the bishops in the States were of Irish origins or descent. Such Irishmen dominated Catholic seminaries and colleges. There were great tensions amongst the diverse Catholic ethnic groups, but there was a great discrimination against all Catholics throughout this time and further beyond.[5]

Two superb Catholics greatly contributed to the growth and development of the Catholic Church in the States, the Bohemian-born St. John Neumann, Bishop of Philadelphia, and the American-born convert St. Elizabeth Ann Seton.[6] Both worked tirelessly in the field of education. Tragically, however, many Catholics at this time failed to integrate themselves in mainstream American culture because they held on to their respective ethnic subculture in the States.

Despite the great contributions that Catholics were render-

---

[5] See J.P. Dolan, *The Immigrant Church: New York Irish and German Catholics, 1815-1865*, Baltimore: Johns Hopkins University Press (1975).
[6] See n. 61.

ing particularly in the fields of education, social service to the poor, and caring for the sick, they continued to be victims of discrimination, prejudice, and persecution. There were outright anti-Catholic political groups, such as the Know Nothings, and organizations, such as the Orange Institution and the Ku Klux Klan, which publicly maligned and acutely mistreated Catholics. Many members of such groups advocated that Catholics carried a secret plan to seize control of the American government and to follow the orders of a foreign power, the Pope.

# CHAPTER TWELVE

# The Ottoman Menace

## 36. Christianity and the Ottoman Turks

(a) The Fall of Constantinople to the Turks in 1453 marked the beginning of the rise of the Ottoman Empire which had been established as a kingdom in 1299. The Turks persisted in their conquests until 1453, when the *Pax Ottomana* was established and Constantinople became their capital. The empire continued to flourish and expand rapidly until 1683, frequently engaging in severe battles with Christians. During this time-frame, the empire expanded toward North Africa and Western Europe. The second siege of Vienna, in 1683, put an end to this expansionist program. Then the empire entered a period of stagnation and internal strife that lasted until 1827.[1]

The Christian victory over the Turks at Lepanto in 1571 was a major temporary setback for them. The Knights of Malta were emboldened by the decline in Turkish power. They attacked Turkish ships in the Mediterranean whenever possible over the next seventy years or so. Several Popes assisted the Knights in their endeavors.

---

[1]　See Lord Kinross, *Ottoman Centuries*, Harper Perennial (1979); C. Glasse, *New Encyclopedia of Islam*, Rowman Altamira (2003); J. Goodwin, *Lords of the Horizon: A History of the Ottoman Empire*, NY: Picador Edition (2003).

A Venetian fleet attacked and destroyed a fleet of Barbary pirates in 1638. War with the enraged Sultan Murad IV was avoided because he was fighting the Persians. The Venetians paid compensation for the loss of the fleet. Things remained under an apprehensive peace until 1644, when the Knights of Malta attacked a Turkish convoy on its way from Constantinople to Alexandria. The convoy was carrying pilgrims to Mecca and members of the Sultan's harem. The Knights carried their prisoners and loot to a small harbor in Crete, a Venetian possession for over four hundred years. The Venetians were accused of complicity with the Knights. Diplomatic negotiations failed. A Turkish armada landed on Crete in June 1644. Venice was promised assistance by the Papal States and Tuscany if war commenced. However, the local Greek population on the island was not well-disposed toward the Venetians. This played a very important role in future years for the Greeks supplied the Turks with food. In the end, Crete exchanged Christian masters for Moslem ones.

The Turks began slowly conquering Crete until the end of August 1646. By this time, the promised European assistance began to arrive in the form of galleys from the Papal States, Tuscany, the Knights of Malta, and Naples. The Turkish fleet was in complete confusion by September, but the allied Christian fleet missed the opportunity for a decisive strike. When the Christian forces finally moved to retake Canea in October, they were forced to return to their bases. The bulk of the Turkish fleet and army returned to Constantinople in November for winter, leaving behind a strong garrison. Venice frantically tried to seek military and financial support from other European powers, most of which were still involved in the Thirty Years War. The arrival of the plague on both sides in the winter of 1646 slowed things until June 1647, when a small Turkish force routed a larger Venetian

army of mercenaries. The conquest of most of the rest of the island
was inevitable. By the beginning of 1648, all of Crete, except for
Candia and a pocket of places on some smaller islands, was in
Turkish hands. The twenty-one year siege of Candia, the longest
in known history, began in May 1648 and lasted until September
1669. Despite the long Venetian blockade of the Dardanelles that
began in 1646, the political unrest in Constantinople, some heavy
defeats of the Turkish forces, the Ottoman wars in eastern and
central Europe, the sporadic reinforcement of the Venetians by
some of the European powers, Candia capitulated and fell to the
Turks on 5th September 1669. It marked the temporary territorial
zenith of the Ottoman Empire. On the other hand, Venice was not
completely defeated in that it came out a victor against the Turks
in the Dalmatian War that same year, making significant gains
by tripling its territory and securing control of the Adriatic.

Venice would again engage the Turks in battle during the
long Morean War, attempting to reestablish itself as one of the
major powers in the Eastern Mediterranean. But it failed to regain
Crete in 1692. The island remained under Ottoman direct control
up to 1897 when it gained autonomy under Ottoman suzerainty.
It was formally united to Greece in 1913.

(b) The Turks conquered Buda, the capital of Hungary, in
1541. It remained under Turkish rule for the next 145 years. In
the meantime, the Turks pushed farther west in Europe. Different Popes and some Catholic Crowns understood the Turks as
being a major threat not only to Christianity but also to western
civilization. One such person was Blessed Innocent XI. Tragically,
at this time, the Turks were supported by Catholic France.

Poland went to war against the Turks in 1672. General Jan
Sobieski defeated them in 1673 at the Battle of Chocim and captured the local fortress. This victory coincided with the death of

Michael I of Poland. Since the Polish Crown was elective, Sobieski was elected King of the Polish-Lithuanian Commonwealth and crowned as Jan III Sobieski in 1676.

The Turks, despite their defeats, did not abandon their dreams of military campaigns. They embarked on a new one in 1683 and besieged Vienna for a second time. It ignited the Great Turkish War, during which so many lives were lost and so much devastation was experienced by all combatants. Sobieski's military prowess shined at the Battle of Vienna, leading a coordinated army comprised mainly of Polish and Austrian troops against the invading Turks under their military leader and grand vizier Merzifonlu Kara Mustafa Pasha. Following the Turkish defeat, Leopold I of Austria decided on a counterattack to expel altogether the Turkish presence in Hungary. But he needed outside help. Consequently, through the efforts of Blessed Innocent XI, the Holy League was formed in early 1684 among Jan III Sobieski of Poland, Leopold I of Austria, and Venice. The Christian counteroffensive, during the spring of 1684, aimed at the re-conquest of all Hungary. Esztergom, Vác, and Pest easily fell to the main Christian army. During the first siege of Buda, which began in July, the Turks managed to fend off the Christian army. Two years later, in June 1686, a much larger army of an expanded Holy League, comprised of German, Hungarian, Croat, Dutch, English, Spanish, Czech, Italian, French, Burgundian, Danish and Swedish soldiers, once again laid siege to Buda. They were led by the brilliant military leader, Prince Eugene of Savoy. The Christian army entered Buda in early September 1686. There followed a ruthless massacre of Muslims and Jews by the Christian army.

After the Second Battle of Mohács in 1687, the Hungarian parliament recognized the Hapsburgs as their hereditary rulers and that the king of Hungary would be crowned during the lifetime of his father. Up till then, the Hungarian Crown had been elective. Then followed the Battle of Zenda in 1697, where the Turks were completely routed out. A peace treaty was signed in Karlowitz in 1699, concluding the Austro-Ottoman War of 1683-1697. The entire Kingdom of Hungary was completely freed of all Turkish presence in 1718. Also, the constrained Hapsburg Counter-Reformation efforts in the seventeenth century reconverted the majority of the kingdom to Catholicism.

CHAPTER THIRTEEN

# Napoleon Bonaparte

## 37. Napoleon

It is impossible to cover the life and innovations of Napoleon Bonaparte[1] in one volume, much less in a few pages. Military academies around the world still study his military campaigns. He shaped European history through his achievements and by reactions to them. His rapport with the Catholic Church held a particular important aspect of his rule.

Napoleon, a baptized Catholic of Italian ancestry, was born in Corsica in 1769. His rise to power was meteoric. He trained as an artillery officer in France and rose quickly in rank during the First French Republic. Having led successful campaigns during the First and Second Coalitions against France, he staged a coup d'état and installed himself as First Consul in 1799. He was proclaimed Emperor of the French by the French Senate five years

---

[1] See D. Chandler, *The Campaigns of Napoleon*, Simon & Schuster (1995); P. Johnson, *Napoleon: A Life*, Penguin Books (2002); G. Fremont-Barnes *et al*, *The Napoleonic Wars: The Rise and Fall of an Empire*, Osprey (2004); T. Astarita, *Between Salt Water and Holy Water: A History of Southern Italy*, W.W. Norton & Company (2005); J. Abbott, *Life of Napoleon Bonaparte*, Kessinger Publishing (2005); P. Alter *et al* (eds.), *Unity and Diversity in European Culture c. 1800*, OUP (2006); P. Dwyer, *Napoleon: The Path to Power 1769-1799*, Bloomsbury (2008).

later. His Napoleonic Wars involved every major European power which, time and again, formed military alliances to defeat him, recognizing his substantive threat to their very existence and his military genius. Napoleon managed to give France a new legal code,[2] reformed the military, inspired millions, and redrew the map of Europe. He toppled monarchs in continental Europe and replaced them with his family members and very close friends. He brought the demise of the Holy Roman Empire, suppressed the Papal States for a while, and imprisoned two Popes.[3]

Napoleon, whether as General or Emperor, invaded most of the Western European countries and Russia. However, the invasion of Russia in 1812 marked a negative turning point from which he never fully recovered. The Sixth Coalition defeated his army at Leipzig in 1813. The Coalition forces invaded France in 1814 and forced him to abdicate and be exiled to the island of Elba. But he escaped Elba the following year, returned to France in power, generated an enormous fear all over Europe, and began his Hundred Days of rule, ending with his thorough defeat at the Battle of Waterloo in June 1815. He was then exiled to the island of St. Helena, where he lived in confinement under the British for the next six years. Rumors stated for almost two centuries that he died from arsenic poisoning. However, medical research in 2007 and 2008 confirmed evidence of a peptic ulcer and gastric cancer as the cause of death.

---

[2]  This is the Code Napoleon. It laid the foundation for the administrative and judicial systems for much of Western Europe.

[3]  Napoleon gave tacit approval of the imprisonment of Pius VI. But he imprisoned Pius VII.

---

## 38. Napoleon and Italy

---

Captain Napoleon was appointed artillery commander of the republication forces for the siege of Toulon in 1793, then occupied by British forces. Though wounded, he managed to capture Toulon. He was promoted to Brigadier General when he was only twenty-four. He was put in charge of the artillery of the French army for Italy. It was during this time that he devised plans to attack Piedmont as part of France's campaign against the First Coalition,[4] realizing that artillery was the key to a sound defense. When Robespierre fell from power in July 1794, ending the dreaded Reign of Terror, Napoleon was put under house arrest. Released within two weeks, he was asked to draw up plans to attack Italian positions under Austria. But in September 1795, he was removed from the list of generals for his refusal to serve in the Vendée campaign. However, royalists in Paris rebelled the following month. Napoleon, through the influence of a friend, was given command of the forces in defense of the Convention in the Tuileries Palace. He used artillery on the royalists and thereby extinguished all threats to the French Convention. As a result, he was launched into sudden fame, being promoted to Commander of the Interior and given command of the Army in Italy. Within weeks he was romantically involved with Josephine de Beauharnais, whom he married in 1796.

---

[4] There were seven Coalitions against France: First Coalition (1792-1797) was comprised of Austria, Prussia, Britain, Spain, and Piedmont; Second Coalition (1798-1801) was comprised of Russia, Britain, Austria, the Ottoman Empire, Portugal, Naples, and the Papal States; Third Coalition (1805) was comprised of Austria, Britain, Russia, and Sweden; Fourth Coalition (1806-1807) was comprised of Prussia, Saxony, and Russia; Fifth Coalition (1809) was comprised of Britain and Austria; Sixth Coalition (1812-1814) was comprised of Britain, Russia, Prussia, Sweden, Austria, and the German States; Seventh Coalition (1815) was comprised of Britain, Russia, Prussia, Sweden, Austria, and the German States.

Napoleon began his first campaign in Italy in the middle of 1796 with a victory against Austria at the Battle of Lodi. He expelled the Austrians from Lombardy. After Austria defeated him at Caldiero, he was victorious at the Battle of the Bridge of Arcole and proceeded to overrun the Papal States. But he disobeyed the orders of the atheist members of the Directory to march against Rome and dethrone Pius VI. Instead, he led his army in March 1797 into Austria and forced it to negotiate the Treaty of Leoben through which France acquired most of northern Italy and the Low Countries. The treaty contained a secret clause which promised Venice to Austria. Then Napoleon conquered Venice, ending its 1,100 years of independence. He authorized the French to plunder Venice. He would do similar acts in all of his campaigns, including looting the Vatican Apostolic Library and the Vatican Museums.

After Napoleon occupied Ancona and Loreto, papal possessions, Pius VI signed the Peace of Tolentino in February 1797. An anti-French riot broke out in Rome the following December and Napoleon's representative in Rome was killed. In retaliation, Napoleon sent General Berthier to march on Rome and proclaim the Roman Republic. The French army arrived in February 1798 and demanded that Pius VI renounce his temporal powers. When the Pope refused to do so, he was dethroned, taken as a prisoner, and harried toward France. He died at Valence in August 1799, but was not buried until the end of January 1800, when Napoleon thought it politically profitable. By then, Napoleon had realized the importance of using religion as a means to gain power among the numerous French Catholics. The Pope was buried without any ceremonies as "Citizen Braschi."[5] After the 1801 Concordat

---

5  Braschi was the Pope's family name.

with the Holy See, the Pope's body was brought to Rome and solemnly buried in February 1802.

The 1801 Concordat between France and the Holy See was another political ploy on the part of Napoleon.[6] Cardinal Ercole Consalvi, Pius VII's Secretary of State, led the Holy See's side of the negotiations. Napoleon's uncle, Joseph Fesch, to be created a Cardinal in 1803, took an active part on the French side. In the end, the Concordat was clearly tilted toward France's side. But, the connection between Paris and Rome was reestablished. The Concordat recognized Roman Catholicism as the religion of the majority of the people of France. The French State insisted to salary Catholic clergy, thereby forcing the Church in France to forfeit all hope for the return of Church property which had been confiscated during the French Revolution. The majority of the dioceses were suppressed and new dioceses, with new boundaries, were established. Napoleon, despite Consalvi's vehement objections, added the provisions of the so-called "Organic Articles" in April 1802. The articles empowered the State to interfere in the Church's inner affairs, to regulate seminaries, to approve the publication of papal decrees and the convocation of Church synods, to give approval to any Church office, to have a civil marriage ceremony before a Church one, to control all Church salaries, and to deal as a criminal act any breach of the articles' provisions. Pius VII futilely protested these provisions which were enforced without any kind of papal say. The Gallican policy was in full force. Papal influence in European affairs had reached the lowest level in centuries.

---

[6] See H.H. Walsh, *The Concordat of 1801: A Study of the Problem of Nationalism in the Relations of Church and State*, CUP (1933); N. Aston, *Christianity and Revolutionary Europe* c. *1750-1830*, CUP (2002).

---

## 39. First Consul Napoleon

---

While on his first campaign in Italy, Napoleon became progressively more influential in French politics. In reaction to criticism of him by French royalists for plundering Italy and their warning that he was aiming at a dictatorship, he sent General Pierre Augereau to Paris to lead a coup d'état and purge the royalists in September 1797. This left the Directory dependent on Napoleon. He returned to Paris as a hero at the end of that year, after concluding the Treaty of Campo Formio. He met with Charles Talleyrand[7] and began preparations to invade Britain. But Napoleon decided to seize Egypt instead, thereby blocking Britain's commercial access to India. He took with him many scientists and scholars.[8]

While en route to Egypt in 1798, Napoleon wrested the island of Malta from the Knights of Malta. His short stay of a few days saw the looting of the treasures of the Maltese island. The French financial and anti-Catholic policies soon led the Maltese, organized by some Catholic priests, to rebel against France and seek British assistance. The French were expelled in September 1800. It was the first successful rebellion against Napoleon that perdured.

---

[7]  Charles Talleyrand was a skilled, resourceful and double-dealing French diplomat who served intermittently from the *Ancien Régime* right through Louis Philippe, thus he also served under Napoleon. Talleyrand was appointed Bishop of Autun in 1788 due to his family's influence. He fled to England in 1792, was expelled from there in 1794, and then lived in the United States until 1796, when he returned to France. He became French Foreign Minister in 1797. Pius VII lifted Talleyrand's excommunication in 1801. However, Talleyrand married the next year and was automatically excommunicated. Emperor Napoleon made him a Prince of the French Empire in 1806. He reconciled with the Catholic Church right before he died in 1838. See J.F. Bernard, *Talleyrand: A Biography*, NY: Putnam (1973); D. Lawday, *Napoleon's Master: A Life of Prince Talleyrand*, London: Jonathan Cape (2006).

[8]  The Rosetta Stone would be discovered during this expedition.

Napoleon's Egyptian campaign met with initial success, but his navy was defeated by Lord Admiral Horatio Nelson at the Battle of the Nile in August 1798. Napoleon successfully invaded the Ottoman province of Damascus, comprised of Syria and Galilee, the following year. Since disease raged havoc in the French army, Napoleon returned to Egypt, where he kept himself informed on European affairs. He learned that France had suffered a series of defeats and his gains in Italy had been practically wiped out. He left Egypt without Paris' permission and headed for France. After he arrived in Paris, he was encouraged to join in a coup against the Directory. Thus, Napoleon became one of the provisional Consuls to administer the government. Next, he outwitted the other two Consuls and got himself elected First Consul, becoming the most powerful person in France.

Napoleon decided to strike again against Austria. His troops crossed the Alps in 1800. He defeated the Austrians at the Battle of Marengo. During the peace negotiations at Lunéville, Austria, heartened by British support, stated it would not recognize France's newly gained territories. Thus, Napoleon ordered the French army to strike Austria again. As a result, the Treaty of Lunéville was signed in February 1801, the Rhineland was reorganized[9] and France gained more territory in Italy. During the same year, Napoleon also established lasting reforms, including centralized administration of the departments, a tax code, higher education, the metric system, and a central French Bank. Furthermore, France and England, both tired of war, signed the short-lived Treaty at Amiens.

Shortly after Haiti throw off the French colonial yoke in 1802, Napoleon sold France's possessions in North America to the

---

[9] See n. 19.

United States, the Louisiana Purchase.[10] He was elected Consul
for life soon thereafter. By this time, the revision of French law,
the Code Napoleon, was well underway. Napoleon personally
contributed to its composition. It was enacted in 1804.

---

### 40. Emperor Napoleon I

---

There were a few plots against Napoleon's life. He used the plot
financed by the exiled Bourbons in early 1804 to consolidate
his power and as an excuse to found another hereditary French
monarchy with himself as emperor. He invited Pius VII to come
to Paris. The Pope was hesitant and so Napoleon sent his uncle,
Cardinal Fesch, to secure the Pope's presence at his imperial
coronation. Napoleon crowned himself emperor on 2nd December 1804 at Notre Dame and then crowned his wife Josephine
as empress. He crowned himself King of Italy in Milan in May
1805. The Third Coalition against France was formed. Though
Napoleon won the Battle of Ulm, his navy suffered a major defeat
the next day at the hands of the British at the Battle of Trafalgar.
The Third Coalition ended with Napoleon's victory at the Battle
of Austerlitz. Austria ceded to France more territory, the Holy Roman Empire was abolished and the German States reorganized.
Napoleon then created the Confederation of the Rhine under
his protection.

The Fourth Coalition was formed in 1806. Napoleon dev-
astated Prussia in October of that year. The Treaties of Tilsit of
July 1807 were signed between France and Russia and between
France and Prussia respectively. Prussia lost half of its territories

---

[10] See n. 34 (b).

and Europe was practically divided between France and Russia. Then Napoleon proceeded to place puppet monarchs on German thrones and established the Duchy of Warsaw with King Frederick Augustus I of Saxony as ruler. But, Napoleon's attempt to put an embargo on Britain by establishing the Continental System, proved unsuccessful. He invaded Portugal in 1807 for not abiding with the blockade. Next, he replaced the King of Spain with his brother Joseph. But, before he could totally subdue Spain during the Peninsular War, Austria again threatened war and Napoleon had to return to France. War in the Iberian peninsula continued and the French began experiencing setbacks against their enemy's army, led by Arthur Wellesley, Duke of Wellington.

Meanwhile Pius VII and Napoleon locked horns again on matters political and religious. Napoleon pushed for the State's control over spiritual matters. The Pope refused to give into the demands where the discipline and the vital interests of the Church seemed threatened. Cardinal Fesch fruitlessly tried to reconcile the two adversaries. Relations between Rome and Paris deteriorated to such an extent that French troops occupied Rome again in February 1808. Napoleon, as King of Italy, then annexed substantial papal territory to his kingdom. Diplomatic relations were broken off. In May 1809, Napoleon decreed that those territories under direct control of the Papal States were part of the French Empire and that the Pope was to be compensated with an annual stipend. The Pope responded by excommunicating Napoleon. In turn, Pius VII was taken prisoner and harried toward France. In the meantime, Napoleon, acting through close supporters, unsuccessfully put undue pressure on the Pope to yield to his demands. He continued to do so throughout the Pope's captivity. In the interim, Napoleon divorced Empress Josephine and married Archduchess Marie Louise, daughter of Francis I of

Austria. The marriage brought more strain between Napoleon and the Pope, and the former imprisoned fifteen Cardinals for refusing to attend and to recognize his second marriage.

The Franco-Russian alliance established in 1807 began to falter. Russia had virtually abandoned the Continental System by 1811. Napoleon threatened Russia with serious consequences if it allied itself with Britain. Napoleon then decided to invade Russia in June 1812. It was a catastrophic decision. The Russians avoided direct contact with the French and retreated further into Russia, scorching the fields and denying the French a means of nourishment. Finally, the two armies engaged one another at the Battle of Borodino in September 1812. Though the French won, the Russians were invigorated. Next, the Russians retreated beyond Moscow, burning the city as they withdrew. They waited for the onset of winter as their ally. Napoleon had to order a forced retreat due to the harsh Russian winter.

The Sixth Coalition against Napoleon was formed in 1813. Despite initial French success, France was defeated at the Battle of Leipzig. Napoleon withdrew to France, encircled by the Coalition forces. Paris was captured in March 1814. Napoleon was forced to abdicate unconditionally on 11th April 1814 at the Peace of Fontainebleau, and exiled to the island of Elba in isolation. The Pope was freed during the Allies' pursuit of Napoleon's forces.

Napoleon escaped Elba in February 1814 and was acclaimed as emperor by the same French army which was sent to intercept him. He then marched on Paris and Louis XVIII fled. The Seventh Coalition declared war on Napoleon. It finished with the Allies' victory at the Battle of Waterloo on 18th June 1815. Subsequently, the Allies' army entered Paris and restored Louis XVIII. Napoleon was imprisoned and then exiled to the island of Saint Helena in the Atlantic Ocean. He died there in 1821.

# Wars for Crowns

# CHAPTER FOURTEEN

# European Wars of Succession

Western Europe of the eighteenth century witnessed a number of Wars of Succession. France was involved in every one of them. However, the French Monarchy itself came to a very violent end before the conclusion of that century.

## 41. The Spanish Crown in Crisis

Charles II was the last Hapsburg King of Spain.[1] He also ruled a good portion of the Italian peninsula, along with Sicily and Sardinia, the Spanish territories in the Low Countries, and Spain's overseas Empire, stretching from Mexico to the Philippines. He was the only surviving son of Philip IV of Spain and his second wife, Mariana of Austria. Charles' birth temporarily relieved the pressure regarding the royal succession. The centuries-old inbreeding between the Hapsburgs of Austria and of Spain gave their children some very serious hereditary weaknesses, such as many miscarriages and still-births, insanity, and physical deformities. Charles II was physically, mentally, and emotionally deficient.

---

[1]  See H. Kamen, *Spain in the Later 17th Century*, NY: Longman (1980); G. Darby, *Spain in the 17th Century*, NY: Longman (1995).

The King was nicknamed "the Hexed" and even he believed this to be true, going so far as to be exorcised.

Charles was four years old when his father died in September 1665. His mother became Regent. However, she was exiled to Toledo after a successful palace coup in 1677, carried out by John of Austria the Younger, an illegitimate son of Philip IV. She returned to the court after John's death in 1679.

Charles II's entire reign was pestered with very serious problems, apart from his personal ones and his unfitness to rule. The economy was stagnant, hunger ruled the land, the power of the monarchy over the various Spanish provinces was extremely weak, and the Spanish Court was full of foreign manipulation and intrigues. The unwise policies of the powerful Gaspar de Guzmán, Duke of Olivares, during the reign of Philip IV, had accelerated the decline of Spanish influence. The vast negative effects of his policies bore their full impact during the reign of Charles II. Spain lost Portugal and the Portuguese colonies, though the Treaty of Lisbon of 1668 ceded the North African enclave of Ceuta to Spain.

Charles II married twice, but was unable to produce an heir. His last will settled the line of succession. Given that he was a relative to both the Austrian Hapsburgs and the French Bourbons, he named as his first choice for heir his great-nephew, Duke Philip of Anjou,[2] and as an alternative, Archduke Charles of Austria. Since it was unthinkable to the European Crowns to have the Spanish Empire under the control of Louis XIV, who was already the most powerful monarch in Europe, they united against France. Then Louis XIV, in February 1701, decreed that should he die without a

---

[2] Philip was a grandson of Louis XIV of France and of Charles' half-sister, Maria Theresa of Spain. In fact Louis XIV himself was an heir to the Spanish throne through his mother, Anne of Austria, daughter of Philip III of Spain.

legitimate heir, Philip of Anjou would become the King of France and forfeit the Spanish throne. Subsequently, Louis XIV occupied several towns in the Spanish Netherlands. The move sparked the War of the Spanish Succession which lasted from 1702 to 1713. It was fought on four continents. The war ended with the Treaties of Utrecht in 1713 and Rastatt in 1714 and confirmed Philip V as the King of Spain, with the proviso that the Spanish and French thrones may never be united. Ironically, the European powers agreed on practically the same terms that they had already agreed upon before they began their brutal war.

---

## 42. The War of the Polish Succession

Jan III Sobieski of the Polish-Lithuanian Commonwealth died in 1697 and the Polish Parliament, the Sejm, elected the Catholic convert[3] Frederick Augustus I, Elector of Saxony, as their next sovereign. His election was backed by Russia and Austria. He assumed the name of Augustus II and intended to change his new throne from an elective to an hereditary Crown.[4]

Augustus II entered the Great Northern War on the side of Denmark and Russia. They fought Charles XII of Sweden. The latter defeated Augustus II at Riga in June 1701, invaded Poland, and captured Warsaw in May 1702. As Swedish troops occupied more of Poland, Augustus II sued for peace, but Charles XII dethroned him and installed Stanislaw I Leszczyński[5] in his

---

[3] Every Polish sovereign had to be of the Catholic Faith.
[4] Though the provisions of the Peace of Augsburg gave Frederick the right to introduce Catholicism as the religion of Saxony, he never did so and Saxony remained Lutheran.
[5] Stanislaw I Leszczyński was the father-in-law of Louis XV of France.

stead in 1704. Then Augustus II allied himself with Russia and continued the war. Next, Charles XII invaded Saxony and forced Augustus II to yield the Polish throne to Stanislaw I in 1706. The latter managed to hold on to the throne until 1709 when Augustus II replaced him with the help of Russia and, for all effects, the Polish-Lithuanian Commonwealth fell under Russian control. Once Augustus II died in 1733, Stanislaw I became King for the second time. This act ignited the War of the Polish Succession.[6] Russia,[7] opposed to any nominee of France and Sweden, and, along with Prussia, backed Austria's nominee, Elector Frederick Augustus II of Saxony, son of the dead king. War broke out in June 1734. Russia and Austria proclaimed Frederick Augustus II as King Augustus III of Poland.

The War of the Polish Succession was substantially fought in Poland, the Rhineland, and Italy between Stanislaw I of Poland, the French and Spanish Bourbons, and Savoy against Augustus III of Poland, Russia, Austria, and Saxony. Britain refused to aid its ally, Austria.

Once Danzig fell to the Russians in June 1734, Stanislaw I fled to France. The war was formally ended by the Treaty of Vienna in 1738 which awarded Stanislaw the Duchy of Lorraine. Poland's fate was determined by foreign powers. The War of Polish Succession was the root which would in time lead to the partitions of Poland in 1772, 1793, and 1795.

France had occupied the Duchy of Lorraine during the War. Duke Francis of Lorraine, who was soon to marry Maria Theresa

---

[6] See J.L. Sutton, *The King's Honor and the King's Cardinal: The War of the Polish Succession*, University Press of Kentucky (1980); P.H. Wilson, *German Armies: War and German Politics, 1648-1806*, Routledge (1998).

[7] At this time, Russia was ruled by Empress Anna, the daughter of Ivan V of Russia and niece of Peter the Great. She had ascended to the Russian throne in 1730 upon the death of the young Emperor Peter II.

of Austria, ceded his Duchy to the ousted Stanislaw I. In return, France recognized the Pragmatic Sanction in 1713 of Charles VI of Austria that ensured his daughter Maria Theresa would succeed to the Austrian throne upon his death. Duke Francis was also promised to inherit the Grand Duchy of Tuscany once the ruling de Medici dynasty was extinguished with the death of Grand Duke Gian Gastone. He died in 1737.

However, the War of the Polish Succession was a prelude to the War of the Austrian Succession which began in 1740.

---

## 43. The War of the Austrian Succession

The War of the Austrian Succession involved almost all the Crowns of Europe. Austria, Britain, Hanover, the Dutch Republic, Saxony,[8] Sardinia and Russia formed one group in opposition to France, the Spanish Bourbons, Prussia, and Sweden.

The phrase, "the War of the Austria Succession," was coined to identify a number of wars.[9] There were two Silesian Wars; an Austro-Saxon War; an Austro-Bavarian War; a Franco-Austrian War, in which England and the Dutch Republic fought on the Austrian side; an Austro-Spanish War, during which Savoy initially fought against Austria and then switched sides; a Swedish-Russian War, where France attempted to neutralize Russia, a potential ally of Austria; and, finally, France's support of the Jacobite Rebellion in 1745, whereby France had hoped to neutral-

---

[8]  Saxony switched sides to Austria in 1743.
[9]  See R.S. Browning, *The War of the Austrian Succession,* Palgrave Macmillan (1995); M.S. Anderson, *The War of the Austrian Succession, 1740-1748,* NY: Longman (1995); C.W. Ingrao, *The Hapsburg Monarchy, 1618-1815,* CUP (2000); R. Okey, *The Hapsburg Monarchy,* NY: St. Martin's Press (2001); M. Hochedlinger, *Austria's Wars of Emergence, 1683-1799,* London: Longman, (2003); Berenger, op. cit.

ize Britain. There were also some ancillary wars in other parts of the world, particularly in North America and India. It is called King George's War in North America, which incorporated the War of Jenkins' Ear with Spain. Britain became involved with the Austrian Succession issue because it was already at war with Spain in North America.

(a) Charles VI of Austria set up the Pragmatic Sanction in 1713 before he had even fathered a legitimate child. Austria was running out of male heirs. Charles VI made a number of concessions so as to have the decree recognized by the European Crowns. The emperor had to ensure that if he had no male heir, a daughter would succeed him as empress in the Hapsburg domains.

Once the emperor was dead in 1740, France was determined to indirectly avail of every opportunity to weaken Austria. Thus, Louis XV and his chief minister, Cardinal de Fleury,[10] supported all those who declared themselves as a candidate for the imperial throne: Charles of Bavaria, Charles Emmanuel III of Savoy, and Augustus III of Saxony. France also supported those who tried to tear away any part of the Hapsburg territories from Maria Theresa.

The pretext of the war was whether Archduchess Maria Theresa of Austria was eligible to succeed Charles VI as the head of the Hapsburg thrones. France and Prussia, in particular, used the Salic Law[11] as a ploy to challenge Hapsburg power.

Charles VI became Emperor in 1711. By that time, he

---

[10] Cardinal André-Hercule de Fleury was one of the few French bishops who published Clement XI's Papal Bull, *Unigenitus*, imprisoned those clergy who refused to adhere to it, and resisted Jansenism and its adherers. Later, in 1738, he urged Clement XII to issue a Papal Bull which prohibited Catholics from becoming Freemasons under pain of excommunication.

[11] The best-known provision of Salic law is agnatic succession, which excludes females from inheriting the throne.

was the only male in the entire House of Hapsburg because the Spanish Hapsburgs ended with the death of Charles II of Spain in 1700. So Charles VI, not yet a parent, took legal and international precautions to ensure that should he have no legitimate male heirs, his oldest daughter would succeed him. The plan was a modification of that of Leopold I, his father. While the War of the Spanish Succession was raging, Leopold I and his two sons, the future emperors Joseph I and Charles VI, signed a Pact in September 1703 which made it possible for a female to ascend the Hapsburg throne if there was no male heir. After Charles VI succeeded his brother Joseph I, who had left two daughters, the former made specific changes in the Pact of 1703, giving precedence to his possible future daughters over his two nieces. The decree was called the Pragmatic Sanction of 1713. The issue dealt specifically with the Hapsburgs' claim to their possessions. Things began rolling from then onwards. Hungary had recognized the House of Hapsburg as its hereditary monarchy after the expulsion of the Turks in 1687. Bohemia had the same setup. The emperor stated that if he had no legitimate male heir, Hungary would revert to an elective monarchy. But, the Hungarian Parliament passed its own Pragmatic Sanction in 1723, whereby Charles VI's elder daughter, Maria Theresa, would become Queen of Hungary if there was no male heir. Meanwhile the emperor spent a lot of time preparing the European powers to accept his daughter as his successor. Yet, since he had always hoped to have a legitimate son and then refused to accept the fact that he would not have one, he never prepared Maria Theresa to succeed him. It seemed that by the end of his life, the emperor had succeeded to convince the European Crowns. But France, Prussia, Bavaria, and Saxony reneged on their pledge and challenged Maria Theresa's claim to the Austrian lands. She had succeeded Charles VI in 1740 as

Queen of Hungary, Croatia, and Bohemia.

(b) There was never a question that a woman would ever be elected Holy Roman Empress. In fact, the husband of Charles VI's niece, Charles Albert of Bavaria, was elected Holy Roman Emperor Charles VII in 1742, the first non-Hapsburg to wear the imperial crown since the fifteenth century. By the time of his election, he had renounced the Pragmatic Sanction and allied himself with the Bourbons of France and Spain, challenging Maria Theresa's claims over the Hapsburg patrimony. He had been crowned King of Bohemia in December 1741 and crowned Holy Roman Emperor in February 1742. Shortly after his imperial coronation, the Austrian army occupied Bavaria and he was forced to flee from Munich to Frankfurt, ending up as a ruler with no land. Frederick II of Prussia came to his rescue, forced the Austrian army to withdraw from Bavaria, and helped him to enter Munich in October 1744, just to die within three months. His son and successor, Maximilian III Joseph, quickly made peace with his cousin, Maria Theresa, and pledged to support her husband, Grand Duke Francis Stephan of Tuscany, in the upcoming imperial election.

(c) Italian soil, mostly occupied by foreign powers, served as a stage for part of the War of the Austrian Succession. Milan was under Austria. Bourbon Naples and Spain joined forces in 1741 to fight Austrian power in northern Italy. Austria, assisted by Britain and Sardinia, forced their enemies to retreat in 1742. Other skirmishes followed, though there was not a clean victory for Austria and its allies. Then France assisted Naples and Spain, but their army was defeated in October 1743. War took a very serious turn in 1744. Austria and Sardinia, each army in its own turn, were defeated by the Neapolitan and Spanish armies, though these failed to become one fearsome army. Genoa entered into a secret treaty with France, Spain, and Naples in March 1745. The following August saw the departure of most of the British troops who were called back to Britain to counteract the second major Jacobite Rebellion, known as the "Forty-Five Rebellion." The absence of British troops took its toll on their allies. The French defeated again the Sardinian army in September. But the complicated politics across the many Italian City-States denied the French any kind of advantage. Furthermore, the peace treaty between Austria and Prussia in 1746 freed more imperial troops to be relocated to Italian soil. Then the Austrian and Sardinian armies closed in on the French. In the end Austria controlled all of northern Italy. Benedict XIV was very concerned about this new reconfiguration of foreign presence in the Italian peninsula.

Holland was another front of the war. The absence of the British troops was felt and the French took occasion to hammer the Austrians and their Dutch allies in 1746. Brussels fell to the French in 1746. What remained of the British army on the continent unsuccessfully tried to divert the French from Holland. The Austrian Netherlands[12] were conquered by France in April 1747, which then turned its army's attention to the United Provinces of Holland. By May 1748, all of the Netherlands was under French control. A relieving Russian army had arrived too late to render any kind of assistance to Austria and Holland.

(d) North America was not spared from the War of Austrian Succession, where it became known as King George's War. It was waged between Britain and France. British troops captured the important French fortress Louisbourg on Cape Breton Island in June 1745. However, when a peace settlement finally arrived, Britain exchanged the fortress with France for the city of Madras,

---

[12] The Austrian Netherlands are essentially equivalent to today's Kingdom of Belgium.

India, to the great chagrin of the British colonies in America.

While the heartland of Europe served as the stage for the power struggle between Austria and Prussia, the subcontinent of India played the same role for the power struggle between Britain and France. It also marked the beginning of European military ascendancy and political intrusion in the subcontinent. Major hostilities began in early September 1746 with the arrival of the French troops by sea near Madras. The port was immediately blockaded. The poorly equipped British garrison surrendered to the French within six days. The Indian army of Anwaruddin Muhammed Khan, coming to the assistance of the British, was easily crushed by the French the following October. The event highlighted the superiority of European soldiers to those of native Indian principalities. Soon more skirmishes between French and British-Indian forces followed. The British were victorious in most of these encounters which took place between 1746 and 1748, but Madras remained in French hands until the peace settlement between the two countries. However, the conflict between the two countries continued indirectly through their involvement in the fighting between the rival claimants to the Indian thrones of Hyderabad and Carnatic. It was a warm-up for the Seven Years War.

(e) The War of the Austrian Succession ended with the Treaty of Aix-la-Chapelle in 1748. Despite the many challenges that Maria Theresa had faced, she succeeded to hold on to most of the Hapsburg patrimony and the Hapsburg-Lorraine dynasty set on the imperial throne. The most enduring effect of the war was that Prussia had proved itself as a nation with a first class, well-disciplined army, and had acquired Silesia.[13] At the Peace

---

[13] Maria Theresa ceded Silesia to Frederick II after the Second Silesian War.

of Dresden of 1745, Frederick II recognized Francis I's imperial election and retained Silesia in accordance with the provisions of the Peace of Breslau in 1742.[14] The end of the war had another long-term effect. It sparked the creation of German dualism between Prussia and Austria. This would ultimately ignite German nationalism and the drive to unify Germany into a single nation. France had failed to disintegrate the Hapsburg possessions. This failure and the outcome of the subsequent Seven Years War, much more than the War of American Independence, was the major cause for France's bleak financial situation in the late eighteenth century. During the Seven Years War, the Austrian Netherlands, southwestern Germany, Bohemia-Moravia and northern-central Italy became theatres of war. They were incapable of defending themselves because their ruling dynasties resided far away or were politically too fragmented to offer effective resistance.

---

## 44. The War of the Bavarian Succession

---

The War of the Bavarian Succession was a very complicated and brief war between Austria and Saxony-Prussia.[15] The war entailed no substantial pitched battles, but there was a significant human casualty due to disease and starvation. The Saxons and Prussians refer to the war as the "Potato War" and the Austrians call it the "Plum Fuss" due to lack of food for the armies of both sides.

---

[14] There was a Third Silesian War which took place between 1756 and 1763. Austria tried to regain Silesia, but Prussia, now supported by Britain which had been Austria's former ally, resisted and kept Silesia.

[15] See P.H. Wilson, *German Armies: War and German Politics, 1648-1806*, Routledge (1998); D. Fraser, *Frederick the Great: King of Prussia*, Fromm International (2001); C.M. Clark. *Iron Kingdom: The Rise and Downfall of Prussia, 1600-1947.* Cambridge: HUP (2006); Berenger, op.cit.; Ingrao, op. cit.; Kann, op. cit.

(a) When the Duke Maximilian III Joseph of Bavaria died childless at the end of 1777, a number of royals laid claim to the dukedom, including Joseph II of Austria. The emperor had taken for his second wife Maria Josepha, sister of Maximilian III Joseph. Though she predeceased her brother by some ten years, the acquisition of territory in the German-speaking States was an essential part of the emperor's policy to expand Hapsburg influence in Central Europe. Joseph II's claim to the Bavarian throne was perceived by Frederick II of Prussia as a direct threat to the Hohenzollern ascendancy in German politics and influence. Both Maria Theresa and Frederick II saw nothing to be gained by pursuing hostilities. But the emperor refused to drop his claim, despite his mother's insistence. Further still, Frederick Augustus I of Saxony[16] wanted to preserve the territorial integrity of the Duchy for his brother-in-law, Charles Augustus, and did not want the Hapsburgs to acquire additional territory on his southern and western borders. France tried to uphold the balance of power. Finally, Catherine II of Russia threatened to intervene militarily on the side of Prussia. This threat forced the emperor to reconsider his position. The tension was defused with the Treaty of Teschen of 1779. Some historians perceive this war as the last of the old-style Cabinet Wars of the *Ancien Régime* because troops moved from one place to another while diplomats journeyed between capitals to resolve their masters' grievances.

(b) The root of the war was the Pragmatic Sanction of 1713 of Charles VI. Most of the German States accepted the Pragmatic Sanction and the idea that Francis of Lorraine, Maria Theresa's husband, would be the next Holy Roman Emperor. But Bavaria and Saxony could impede Francis's election. When Charles VI

---

[16] Frederick Augustus I was Prince-Elector of Saxony from 1763 to 1805, King of Saxony from 1806 to 1827, and Duke of Warsaw from 1807 to 1813.

died in 1740, his daughter Maria Theresa had to fight for her family's rights to Bohemia, Hungary, and Croatia, and her husband faced competition in his election as the Holy Roman Emperor.

Charles Albert of Bavaria claimed the Hapsburg German territories as a son-in-law of Joseph I. He also presented himself as Charles VI's legitimate imperial successor. He argued that if Hapsburg women were to inherit, then the crown should pass to his wife, Maria Amalia, daughter of Joseph I, Charles VI's older brother. He found support from Prussia, France, and Spain, each of which had different reasons for doing so. All these Crowns reneged on the Pragmatic Sanction. Charles Albert managed to get himself elected Emperor, but without the Hapsburg possessions. When he died in 1745, Maria Theresa's husband succeeded him on the imperial throne. Benedict XIV purposefully stayed out of the picture.

(c) France supported the rebellion against Britain in North America. A major change in French foreign policy in 1756 abandoned the anti-Hapsburg position. France and Austria became allies. The new policy was sealed with the marriage of the French Dauphin Louis[17] and Archduchess Marie Antoinette, daughter of Maria Theresa, in 1770. But France managed to extricate itself from immediate military obligations in 1778 when Joseph II occupied Bavaria. The occupation was unacceptable to Prussia, which mobilized its troops near the borders of Bohemia. France informed Austria it would not be involved in a war against Prussia. Britain, on the other hand, was already deeply involved in the War of American Independence. Though none of the European

---

[17] Louis XVI, the last French King before the French Revolution, reigned as King of France and Navarre from 1774 until 1791, then as King of the French from 1791 to 1792. He was the only French King ever to be executed, an event which took place on 21st January 1793.

countries had fully recovered from the effects of the recent Seven Years War, war was in the air. Despite frantic diplomatic efforts to defuse the situation, two vast Austrian and Prussian armies faced one another by early Spring 1778. They carried the potential of another major war. Prussia was ready to invade Bohemia by April and diplomatic negotiations were ended.

(d) One of the distinguishing marks of the War of the Bavarian Succession was that it was a war of successive skirmishes, with no pitched battles. The first one took place in July 1778 when the Prussians crossed into Bohemia with several hundred soldiers. A rather insignificant Bohemian captain of cavalry and his fifty Hussars tricked the Prussians into believing that they were friendly, and defeated the much surprised Prussian troops. Frederick II of Prussia invaded Bohemia a few days later. The main Austrian army went on red alert on the heights of the Elbe River and a smaller army guarded the passes from Saxony and Lusatia into Bohemia. Next followed a number of raids and counter-raids by both armies which then settled into a stalemate. Their greatest common enemy was the lack of food for the troops and lack of forage for their horses. In the end, it was two empresses who defused the tension and brought on a settlement. Maria Theresa of Austria secretly enlisted the assistance of Catherine the Great of Russia. The latter accepted the offer as mediator. After a few more skirmishes between the two armies, both sides sued for peace, which was enacted by the Treaty of Teschen in 1779. The six-month war without battles turned out to be very costly for both sides in terms of human lives and monetary expenses. But the underlying problem which led to this war was not resolved. Joseph II's foreign policy of expanding Hapsburg influence over German-speaking territories continued to be seen as a threat by Frederick II. When, in 1785, Joseph II sought again to push

Charles IV Theodore to exchange territory, Frederick II renewed his offer to aid the Prince-Elector. However, this time matters were resolved through political pressures on Joseph II. Eventually Bavaria passed to Maximilian IV Joseph, brother of Charles II Augustus, who would rule as Prince-Elector of Bavaria from 1799 until 1805 and as King Maximilian I of Bavaria from 1806 until his death in 1825.

# Popes and Internal Church Governance

# CHAPTER FIFTEEN

# Popes Governing the Papal States

## 45. The Dual Role of a Pope

Every Pope has a dual identity. One belongs to the exclusively spiritual sphere and the other to the temporal sphere. Even today, Benedict XVI is not only the Bishop of Rome and the Universal Pastor of the Catholic Church but also the temporal sovereign of the autonomous country of Vatican City State. In the past, Popes were absolute rulers of the Papal States in temporal matters up to 1870.[1]

One of the major responsibilities of a Roman Pontiff is to govern not only the Universal Church and promote Church unity in doctrine and morals and confirm his brethren in their Faith, but also to govern the then Papal States. Thus Popes, down the centuries, have carried out this dual role through calling General Councils, local Synods, consultations on diverse decrees and entrusting specific issues and projects to trustworthy individuals, close friends, and even relatives. It is understandable that at times a choice of a specific papal counselor proved to be a major mistake in papal judgment.[2] For example, a dark cloud will remain over

---

[1] See Spiteri, *At Your Fingertips* I, nn. 19, 21, 22.
[2] Such decisions have nothing to do with Papal Infallibility because they do not involve papal teachings in matters of faith and morals.

the pontificate of Innocent X for allowing his widowed sister-in-law, Olimpia Maidalchini, to wield overwhelming power in the running of the papal curia and the Papal States.[3]

---

### 46. Nepotism

---

For a number of centuries, Popes practiced nepotism[4] with little success by way of exception, as was the case with Pius IV.[5] The practice of creating Cardinal-nephews dated back to the Middle Ages but reached its zenith in the sixteenth and seventeenth centuries when their office had almost plenipotentiary powers, second only to that of the Pope himself. The history of nepotism during these centuries had its ups and downs.

Cardinal Fabio Chigi was elected as Alexander VII in April 1655. When he was papal representative at the Peace of Westphalia, he declined to deliberate with heretics and then protested against the Treaty which, in effect, established a new balance of European power that lasted until the French Revolution. The Cardinal entered the conclave as Spain's favorite candidate and was elected Pope after eighty days. One of Cardinal Chigi's appealing qualities to the Cardinal-Electors was his strong opposition to the then prevalent nepotism. Then, to everyone's amazement, the new Pope announced, within three weeks of his election, that he was calling his brother and nephews to assist him in Rome.

---

[3] See P. Levillain (ed.), "Innocent X," op. cit.; Spiteri, *At Your Fingertips* III, n. 19 (e).

[4] See G. Signorotto and M.A. Visceglia, *Court and Politics in Papal Rome*, CIP (2002); R. Hsia, *The World of Catholic Renewal, 1540-1770*, CUP (2005); E. Duffy, op. cit.

[5] The Cardinal-nephew was Charles Borromeo. See Spiteri, *At Your Fingertips* III, n. 35 (a).

The papal administration was chiefly handed over to his relatives and nepotism began to triumph again. He created as Cardinal his nephew Flavio Chigi in April 1657 and gave him the run of the general affairs of the Holy See. Another nephew, Sigismundo Chigi, was created Cardinal the following December.

Alexander VII's successor, Clement IX, generally shunned nepotism and did very little, if anything, to advance his relatives. But, there seems to have been a need to restore some form of nepotism under Clement X, who had turned eighty during the conclave which elected him Pope in April 1670. His niece, Laura Caterina Altieri, was the only heir to carry the family name and the Pope wanted it to survive. Thus, he adopted the Paluzzi family on the proviso that one of their members would marry Laura and take the Altieri name and the uncle of the groom, Cardinal Paluzzo Paluzzi, be named Cardinal-nephew. The latter proved to be a rogue and a tyrant. He alienated the local community and managed to evoke great ire from ambassadors to the Holy See through heavy taxation on all goods. The Pope was forced to refer Paluzzi's financial dealing to a papal committee to pacify the ambassadors and their masters.

Nepotism was out of favor under Blessed Innocent XI, but swung back with Alexander VIII, who put the Holy See in dire financial straits in his very short reign. He reversed the policy of the former, handling charities haphazardly on a huge scale and his nepotism knew no bounds. He created as Cardinal his grand-nephew Pietro Ottoboni in 1689, right after his papal election, bestowing upon him many affluent Church offices. He appointed his nephew Antonio as Commander of the papal forces, and another grand-nephew, Marco, as the first Duke of Fiano. He also revived the sinecure offices, which had been suppressed by Blessed Innocent XI, to provide his relatives with a title that generated lots of income but required insignificant or no work.

The pendulum of nepotism swung back with Innocent XII. He issued the Papal Bull *Romanum decet Pontificem*,[6] on 22$^{nd}$ June 1692, in an attempt to give a fatal blow to the practice. The papal document prohibited all future Popes from bestowing any new acquisitions or source of income on any relative, save to one qualified relative who could be made a Cardinal. Yet, only three of the eight Popes during the eighteenth century did not create a relative as a Cardinal. But, there is another side to the practice in that the College of Cardinals seemed to prefer papal governance through Cardinal-nephews than by papal favorites. For example, the Cardinals, soon after the papal election of Gregory XIII, urged the Pope to appoint his nephew Filippo Boncompagni as Cardinal-nephew. The Pope did so in June 1572. The second instance was under Benedict XIII who was urged by many Cardinals to appoint a Cardinal-nephew to replace the decadent and corrupt Cardinal Niccolò Coscia.

---

## 47. Cardinals Secretary of State

(a) Although the Cardinal-nephew Neri Corsini of Clement XII reached extraordinary heights, the beginning of the decline of the power of Cardinal-nephews began in the eighteenth century as the role of the Secretary of State began to rise in prominence. Benedict XIV was once described as a sovereign who had neither favorites nor nephews. Some forty years later, after the long conclave of 1800, the new Pope, Pius VII, shunned the office of Cardinal-nephew and relied heavily on his Cardinal Secretary of

---

6   The Papal Bull began with the phrase, "It befits the Roman Pontiff."

State, Ercole Consalvi. Gregory XVI was the only Roman Pontiff who created a Cardinal-nephew, Gabriele della Genga Sermattei, in the nineteenth century. The new Cardinal was the nephew of Leo XII, and so he was not a Cardinal-nephew in the strict sense. When Pius IX lost his temporal power over the Papal States in 1870, many of the structural conditions which had played a major role with family politics during the pontificates of earlier Popes simply evaporated, though there were some exceptions under Leo XIII in 1879 and Pius XII after 1944.

(b) The Cardinal Secretary of State for Pius IV was his nephew, Charles Borromeo, a saint. The Holy See's office of Cardinal Secretary of State, when it was not occupied by a Cardinal-nephew, evolved progressively from the role formerly held by Cardinal-nephews. One invariably checked the power of the other when two different men occupied the respective offices. As more career-oriented bureaucrats in the papal court grew in number under a papal centralized administration, the need for Cardinal-nephews became less important and the star in power of a Cardinal Secretary of State began rising proportionately.

---

## 48. Church Renewal and Reforms

(a) Innocent X had some impressive success in the field of religion and education. He raised the Colegio de Santo Tomas in Manila, the Philippines, to a University in 1645. Five years later saw the celebration in Rome of the Jubilee Year 1650. Some three million pilgrims went to Rome. Many walked over the new inlaid floors inside St. Peter's Basilica and were rapt by the beauty of its bas-reliefs and by Bernini's new Fontana dei Quattro Fiumi in

Piazza Navona. By this time, Rome had established itself as the mistress of Baroque.

Clement IX was very pastoral. He heard confessions twice a week at St. Peter's Basilica, visited hospitals, and assisted the poor whenever he could. He hoped his personal life would inspire others to do the same. Blessed Innocent XI took measures to correct clerical abuse and worldliness, inspiring both clergy and laity to lead a simple moral life by his personal simple lifestyle. Innocent XII, being solicitous of the poor, turned part of the Lateran Palace into a hospital for the needy, and established many charitable and educational institutions.

Benedict XIII was known for his asceticism and continued to follow this regimen after his papal election. He, through the provincial Lateran Council of 1725, began reforming the worldly Italian hierarchy. He consecrated so many bishops from around the world that the majority of today's episcopal hierarchy can trace their episcopal lineage back to him. Alas, though acting in his spiritual capacity, he caused an international incident when he promoted the Office of the Hours of St. Gregory VII, which contained an account of the excommunication and deposition of Emperor Henry IV.

Benedict XIV reformed the education of priests, canon law, the calendar of Church feasts, the episcopal ceremonial book, numerous papal institutions which included the papal nobility, and the process of beatification and canonization, to name a few. He approved the founding of the Passionists by St. Paul of the Cross and of the Redemptorists by St. Alphonsus Maria Liguori. The two congregations would bring a renewal in the spiritual life of the Church. His successor, Clement XIII was already famous for his charity toward the needy before his papal election. He continued to do so after he became Pope, using his personal funds and those of the Holy See.

Pius VII restored the Society of Jesus. Soon thereafter, the Jesuits, sensing great papal support, began buying much property which was destined for colleges and seminaries. They pushed for a spiritual and educational renewal.

Leo XII, a great reactionary, reorganized the educational system and placed it exclusively under clerical control. He issued endless regulations on private and public matters. He went against the ladies' fashion of the day, attaching penalties for wearing offending garments and for those who made them. As more secret societies were expanding in the Papal States, he recruited Jesuits to help counteract them. Thus, he gave the Society of Jesus substantial donations and several buildings in Rome, such as the Roman College and the Church of St. Ignatius. He strongly supported their educational endeavors.

Pius VIII instituted some reforms in the Papal States. He confronted the heresy of religious pluralism. He condemned Masonic secret societies, not only those that were in Rome but throughout Christendom. On the other hand, Gregory XVI, like the rest of Europe, was faced with the issue of democratic and modernizing reforms. He judged them to be excuses from the revolutionary left. To counteract these, he took measures to strengthen the political and religious authority of the Papacy. Thus, he tacitly promoted Ultramontanism. The original meaning of the term was innocent enough, someone who comes from beyond the mountains. But the meaning of the term underwent a radical change after the Protestant Reformation. In France it meant a Catholic who supported papal authority in French political affairs, thus opposing Gallicanism and Jansenism. By the seventeenth century, the term usually became associated with the Jesuits for defending the superiority of the Pope over every kind of Council and over all monarchs, even in temporal matters. When Febronianism and Josephism emerged, it was applied to Catholics who supported the Pope against the policies of the States within the Holy Roman Empire. The basic argument its proponents put forward was that since the Pope enjoyed supreme authority in the Universal Church, then the entire Church should be immune to any outside interference.

Pius IX was initially perceived by the Romans as a liberal Pope and a great change from the repressive Gregory XVI. He gave into the people's call for general amnesty to all political prisoners and grudgingly acceded to their demand to expel the Jesuits from Rome. The released prisoners simply resumed their subversive activities. Members of the ultramontanist movement stood by in disgust. Pius IX mistakenly concluded that he was in control... until 1848, when revolutions broke all over Europe, including in the Papal States. His flight from Rome was followed by the declaration of his deposition as head of the Papal States and the temporary establishment of another Roman Republic.

(b) Some fiscal reforms were a success and others completely failed. Innocent X almost caused a war between Rome and France when he initiated punitive legal proceedings against two Barberini Cardinals, his predecessor's nephews.[7] They were charged with misappropriation and abuse of public funds. The two Cardinals fled to France and sought the protection of Cardinal Mazarin. The Pope also supplied financial assistance to Venice and the Knights of Malta in the drawn-out siege of Crete by the Turks, and aided the Irish Catholics with both military

---

[7] See Spiteri, *At Your Fingertips* III, n. 19 (d) (e).

equipment and money during the English Civil War.

Blessed Innocent XI's family background in banking and business proved to be a great asset when reforming the decadent Roman practice of providing family and friends with huge financial resources. Thus, he reformed the Roman administrative organism and abolished the sinecure system. Yet, abuse crept in again under his successor, Alexander VIII. The latter's policy was reversed by Innocent XII, who checked the simoniacal practice at the Roman Curia and introduced further financial reforms along the line of Blessed Innocent XI. But, the papal finances were a fiasco under Benedict XIII. He mistakenly entrusted Church government to Cardinal Niccolò Coscia, who had been his secretary when he was Archbishop of Benevento. Coscia was a corrupt churchman whose embezzlement practices ruined the papal treasury and brought to a very low ebb the Papacy's prestige. The hated Coscia fled Rome after the election of the new Pope, Clement XII. He was subsequently prosecuted, temporarily imprisoned and deprived of the cardinalate, and made to pay a hefty fine.

Clement XII had a great grasp of finances. He found it necessary to rescue the papal treasury from its financial woes. Consequently, he revived the public lottery and, through it, gained a steady source of income which allowed him to undertake extensive building and restoration programs for which he is chiefly remembered, but which he was never able to see. Further financial reforms were undertaken by Benedict XIV. He almost succeeded in eradicating usury in Rome. He reorganized the division of Rome so as to introduce better administrative efficiency. He promoted new agricultural methods and commerce so as to rescue the depleted papal treasury due to Cardinal Coscia's abuses and the enormous costly building and restoration undertakings of Clement XII.

The initial years of Pius VI showed promise in reforming the corrupt administration of the Papal States. Prince Potenziani, the governor of Rome, was reprimanded for failing to deal adequately with local corruption. Nicolò Bischi was called on the carpet for mishandling funds intended to buy grain. In order to boost agriculture in the Papal States, the Pope instituted a reward system based on merit. He denied an annual pension to some prominent people. Furthermore, he appointed a Council of Cardinals to find a means to redeem the ruinous financial condition of the Papal States.

Pius VII, soon after his arrival in Rome in July 1800, embarked on a reform program which had been envisioned by Pius VI. Part of the reform was the economic recovery of the Papal States. The pre-republic system of Church government was restored with some major changes. These included the entry of some noble laymen in administrative positions, the simplification of procedures, the reorganization of tribunals, free trade in grain and food supplies, and a new currency. The following year, 1801, saw the fiscal reform in the taxation system. The greatest resistance came from Cardinals and the Roman nobility. The reforms went aground before Cardinal Consalvi, the then Secretary of State, was forced out of office in 1806. After the Pope returned to Rome from his forced exile, he re-instated Cardinal Consalvi and turned once again to reform and to reorganize the administrative and judicial arms of the Papal States. But the Carbonari kept calling for constitutional reforms and Italian unity. The Pope issued condemnations of this and similar secret societies, becoming a pawn in Metternich's overall European policy. The feudal system in Rome began its gradual disappearance in 1818 as a policy of economic modernization took hold.

Leo XII dismissed Cardinal Consalvi as Secretary of State and began dismantling the policies of Pius VII. He reformed the judicial system in that he made the rendering of justice less costly. Some public improvements were made at such an expense that the Holy See's finances were in chaos, and even the jubilee of 1825 did not generate enough income to adequately cover financial obligations. He put all charitable institutions within the Papal States under direct supervision. His reforms were so ruinous that there were many rebellions and assassinations across the Papal States.

Gregory XVI and his Secretary of State, Cardinal Luigi Lambruschini, opposed basic industrial innovations such as gas lighting and railways because they concluded that such things would promote liberal reforms that would weaken the monarchical papal power. However, he did not spare any money for defensive, architectural and engineering works. These activities contributed to further debilitate papal finances. Blessed Pius IX inherited his predecessor's multi-faceted problems which he had to confront. He was perceived as a liberal Pope who could rescue the Holy See. At the time, most of Europe considered the Papal States stood in urgent need of reform in the areas of local government, finance, administration, and justice. In the meantime, Austria maintained its hold over the Italian peninsula with the excuse that it was peppered with rebellious Italian nationalists. Then came 1848, the year of the revolutions, which would upset the balance of power in Europe. The Pope tried to prevent revolution in Rome by appointing popular ministers, but none of them could defuse the local revolutionary spirit. The situation got so bad that he fled to Gaeta in the Kingdom of Naples. When he returned to Rome, his liberal attitude was gone.

## 49. Ecumenical Efforts

Alexander VII witnessed the conversion to the Catholic Faith of the young Lutheran Queen Christina of Sweden. Her price was to abandon the Swedish throne in 1654. The Pope welcomed her to Rome, where she stayed as a papal guest until her death in 1689. He hoped her conversion would propel other Protestant sovereigns to convert to Catholicism. There was no response.

Clement XII made some strides in the area of ecumenism by protecting Church doctrine and reaching out to Orthodox Churches. He strongly opposed Jansenism, succeeding in procuring the submission of the Maurists to the contents of *Unigenitus*. He was the first Pope to condemn Freemasonry through a Papal Bull of 28th April 1738 entitled *In eminenti*. He received the Patriarch of the Coptic Church into union with Rome. He persuaded the Armenian Patriarch to lift his Church's ancient anathema against the Council of Chalcedon and St. Leo the Great. He founded in Calabria a college for Greek students, the Ullano. He summoned to Rome the Greek-Melkite monks of Mount Lebanon and gave them the ancient Church of Santa Maria in Domnica. He sent the prominent scholar Joseph Simeon Assemani to the East to search for manuscripts and to preside as Papal Legate at the national council of the Maronites. He also established a Maronite college in Rome. He showed decent toleration of Protestants in the Papal States. He naively issued a Papal Bull in 1732 for the Protestants of Saxony, where the rulers were Catholic since 1697, assuring them that if they converted they would not lose the Catholic possessions they had gained from the secularization of Church lands.

The Wars of Religion were history.[8] Much of the bitterness between Catholics and Protestants had worked itself out in many places. Since Catholics and Protestants were marrying one another, there was a call, particularly in Holland and Poland, that such marriages be recognized by Rome. Benedict XIV decreed in June 1748 that such marriages would be recognized if certain conditions were met, in particular that children from such unions be raised as Catholic. Decisions like this created a less hostile setting toward the Catholic Church in Protestant countries. But, he never lost sight of the essential mission, interests and rights of the Church. He sent the pallium to Seraphim Tanas in 1774 and recognized him as Cyril VI, Patriarch of the Catholic Greek Melkites in Antioch. The conflicts with the Maronite Church which seriously threatened its unity after the deposition of Jacob II Awad, were settled at a national council in 1736, the decrees of which the Pope approved. Furthermore, he prohibited activity that aimed to Latinize members of the Eastern Catholic Churches.

The Protestant Elector of Brandenburg declared himself King Frederick I of Prussia in 1701, severing all dependence on Poland. Benedict XIV had to deal with his grandson, Frederick the Great. The King had annexed Catholic Silesia in 1741 and began to impose civil legislation on Silesia's Catholics in marriage laws, as well as Church benefices and jurisdiction. After lengthy negotiations, the Pope and the King reached an uneasy accommodation in 1748, and Benedict even recognized Frederick II as King, despite major opposition from the Roman Curia. Still,

---

8   See N.M. Sutherland, *Princes, Politics and Religion, 1547-1589*, London: Hambledon Press (1984); R.J. Knecht, *The French Religious Wars*; idem., *The French Civil Wars (Modern Wars in Perspective)*, Harlow (2000); Spiteri, *At Your Fingertips* III, nn. 44 (c) to 45 (a).

the European public praised the Pope for his willingness to seek accommodation with a Protestant absolute ruler.

The Holy See's relationship with other Christian Churches did not go well under Pius VIII. He affirmed that the Catholic Church is superior and stands alone above any other Christian Church. He condemned translations of the Bible into the vernacular when accompanied with commentaries which were not faithful to the official Catholic teachings and discipline. On the other hand, he was flexible in accepting mixed marriages between Catholics and Protestants in Germany, but was against liberalizing tendencies in both Ireland and Poland.

When Gregory XVI was Cardinal, he negotiated the adjustment of the Concordat with the Protestant Kingdom of the Netherlands, promoting the interests of the Catholics in Wallonia. In addition, he negotiated peace on behalf of Armenian Catholics with the Ottoman Empire. He was also sent as papal envoy to deal with the Russian Orthodox Nicholas I of Russia who, in his capacity as Tsar, was also King of Poland. He had a policy of suppressing non-Russian nationals, and religions in particular. Thus, he suppressed the Greek Catholic Churches in the Ukraine and Belarus and began forcing Catholic Polish boys to convert to Russian Orthodoxy. The Cardinal tried to win favor with the Tsar by discouraging Catholic Polish revolutionaries from undermining the Tsar's efforts to support the Catholic royalist cause in France.

# CHAPTER SIXTEEN

# Meddling in Papal Elections – Veto Powers

## 50. Electing a Pope

The procedure of electing the Roman Pontiff, the Pope, has undergone some major developments since the Lord directly appointed St. Peter. The last change happened in 2007 when the current Pope, Benedict XVI, reinstated the requirement of two-thirds majority alone for a canonically valid papal election. The current procedure is essentially similar to the one laid out at the Council Lyon II in 1274 in response to the previous long interregnum.[1]

In ancient times, the Bishop of Rome, like any other bishop, was chosen by the clergy and the approval of the laity of the diocese with the assistance of bishops from neighboring dioceses. The method frequently proved to be rather imprecise in that there were some instances when two rivals were elected. In order to avoid confusion, the Roman Emperor, by now a Catholic, sometimes confirmed a papal election. This, perhaps accidentally, provided the possibility

---

[1] An interregnum is the time between the death of one Pope and the election of his successor. The longest interregnum lasted from the death of Clement IV on 29th November 1268 to the election of his successor, Blessed Gregory X on 1st September 1271. Even with the new rules, there was another long interregnum during the same century. It lasted from the death of Nicholas IV on 4th April 1292 until the election of St. Celestine V on 5th July 1294. Other long interregnums were from 20th April 1314 to 7th August 1316, and from 4th July 1415 to 11th November 1417.

for eventual interference of secular rulers in papal elections.

The Lateran Synod of 769 officially abolished the approval of the laity as a part of the protocol of a papal election. But, the Synod of Rome of 862 restored the participation of Roman noblemen. Moreover, each new Pope had to take an oath of loyalty to the Holy Roman Emperor.

Nicholas II introduced a major change in papal elections in 1059. Cardinals were to be the only persons involved in electing a Pope. The procedure was rather straightforward: the Cardinal-Bishops were to meet after the death of the Pope in order to discuss a possible successor. Then the Cardinal-Priests and Cardinal-Deacons were summoned and the three sets of Cardinals voted. The Pope took office after receiving the assent of the clergy and the laity in Rome. The imperial confirmation of the new Pope was abrogated. Next, Council Lateran II of 1139 removed the procurement of the assent of the lower clergy and the laity. Today, since the number of Cardinal-Electors is so large,[2] one might get the wrong impression that procedures in papal elections were always this clear-cut.

During much of the Middle Ages and the Renaissance the usual number of Cardinals was less than thirty and their number dropped as low as seven during the pontificate of Alexander IV. Bad traveling conditions also reduced the number of Cardinals attending a conclave either because they were too sick to travel or because an enormous distance prohibited them to arrive in time to cast their vote. Therefore, each vote became significant and was not usually detached from family or political interests. Cardinals were not sequestered at this time and could come and go at pleasure

---

[2]  Sixtus V fixed the maximum number of Cardinals to seventy in 1587. Paul VI, in 1970, set the limit to one hundred and twenty and decreed that Cardinals over eighty were ineligible to vote at a conclave.

during a given conclave. Thus, there were times when a conclave took months or even years. The long interregnum that followed the death of Clement IV in 1286 caused his successor, Gregory X, to decree at the Council of Lyons II in 1274 that the Cardinal-Electors were to be sequestered, and that their food be reduced after eight days in conclave. John XXI suspended these restrictions and lengthy conclaves continued until 1294. When the hermit Pietro Morrone chastised the Cardinal-Electors during the 1294 conclave, they turned around and elected him as (St.) Celestine V. His notable acts during his very brief pontificate were to re-impose the strict conclave and to resign the Papacy. The election of Urban VI and its shameful aftermath of the Great Western Schism have been discussed in an earlier volume of this series.[3] When Martin V was elected in 1451 and ended the Great Western Schism, he decreed that no General Council had any authority over a Roman Pontiff and that a papal election could never be undone.

The Catholic Counter-Reformation came to an end in most of Europe with the Peace of Westphalia in 1648. Although the inner reform of the Catholic Church was an ongoing sober process, it did not mean that problems simply disappeared. There were abuses within the Church as well as abuses inflicted on the Church by secular authorities. For example, the appalling system of papal nepotism was not completely eradicated for a long time, though it was certainly curtailed under a number of papacies. However, one of the major abuses inflicted by secular rulers was the sheer political maneuverings which went on during the majority of papal elections during the period being covered in this volume. Though the prestige of the papacy frequently fluctuated in its value throughout this time-frame, the fact remained that a

---

[3]   See Spiteri, *At Your Fingertips* I, n. 59; idem., *At Your Fingertips* II, n. 2.

Pope was the spiritual leader of tens of millions of people across the globe. Papal policies and decisions did not only affect the spiritual realm but also the respective political life of various nations, especially those which were Catholic. Consequently, many Catholic sovereigns perceived the occasion of a conclave as an event in which they could attempt to control a specific papal election for sheer secular political motives and with an eye on future papal policies. They did so by vetoing specific *papabili*[4] as well as by presenting their expectations of the new pontificate through their Crown-Cardinals.

## 51. Veto Powers at Papal Elections

(a) In ancient times, Popes used to wait for the Roman Emperor to confirm their papal election. Sometimes the imperial response took long in coming. It all depended on what the Emperor happened to be doing at the time or on the current traveling conditions. Eventually Popes began to simply inform the Emperor of their election. But there was never a time during Imperial Rome or Byzantium when an Emperor deposited a direct veto against a specific *papabile*, though there were occasions when some Roman Emperor or a powerful Roman baronial family or a Holy Roman Emperor imposed his preferred candidate on the papal throne.[5] On the other hand, the emergence of Crown-Cardinals[6] from the time of the end of the Great Western Schism brought with it further secular interference in papal elections which reached its apex in the direct veto of a *papabile* in the name of a secular prince. It is inconceivable

---

[4] A *papabile, papabili* in plural, is a person who is considered as a possible Pope.
[5] See Spiteri, *At Your Fingertips* I, nn. 25 (b), 27.
[6] See L.J Spiteri, *The Emerging Role of the Cardinals and Papal Elections*, Vatican City (2007); idem., *At Your Fingertips* II, nn. 25-26.

today to think that any secular power can directly and specifically exercise such blatant and shameful interference in the election to the highest office in the Catholic Church and in the exercise of an act that totally and exclusively belongs to the spiritual sphere. Yet, Hapsburg Spain raised a claim in 1605 that its sovereign had a right to veto any *papabile*.[7] The veto claim, called *ius exclusivae*,[8] was later taken up by Spain, France, and the Holy Roman Empire. These three monarchies, and later by Austria after the abolition of the Holy Roman Empire, utilized their imposed entitlement to veto a *papabile* through their respective Crown-Cardinals in almost all of the papal conclaves until 1903.

(b) The royal claim was, in all effects, a usurpation of power by secular authorities. The Papacy never formally recognized the veto but it was regrettably tolerated as being an unavoidable abuse. In any case, different Popes issued directives to counteract this disgraceful abuse. Gregory XV prohibited Cardinal-Electors in 1621 to scheme at excluding any papal candidate. Blessed Pius IX, in 1871, forbade any kind of secular interference in papal elections. Finally, St. Pius X, who was probably elected Pope due to the Austrian veto against Cardinal Mariano Rampolla, absolutely and specifically forbade the *jus exclusivae* in the Constitution, *Commissum Nobis*, of 20th January 1904, stating that a Cardinal would incur an automatic excommunication when posting such a veto. Since then every Cardinal-Elector at all subsequent conclaves takes a solemn oath that he in no way, shape or form, directly or indirectly, is voting with deference to any secular power. However, it goes without saying that many heads of secular States continue to show an acute interest in papal elections due to the worldwide influence of the Papacy.

---

[7]   Spain subsequently posted its first veto during the 1644 conclave.

[8]   The Latin term *ius exclusivae* means "the right of exclusion."

## 52. The First Papal Veto

Spain was the first nation which, during both conclaves of 1605, raised the issue that its King could express his will through a Cardinal-Elector to exclude a specific *papabile* during a conclave. The issue remained on the theoretical level until the conclave of 1644.

The pro-French Urban VIII died in July 1644. He left behind him an excessive debt. His entire pontificate had unfolded during the Thirty Years War. During this period, Cardinal Richelieu[9] was determined to make France replace Austria's dominance in Europe. The Pope was distinctly sympathetic toward France and unfavorable to the Hapsburg Crowns. His deep fear of Hapsburg domination in Italy forced him to have a pro-French policy.

Richelieu was succeeded by Cardinal Mazarin[10] as French Prime Minister in 1642. At this time, Mazarin had to address trouble at home and war abroad. He deemed it of utmost importance that the new Pope was not pro-Hapsburg and had to find a way to block the election of such a papal candidate. He decided to go personally to the conclave and post France's veto. But he arrived too late.

Members of the House of Hapsburg ruled both the Holy Roman Empire and the vast Spanish Empire. Ferdinand III succeeded his father Ferdinand II in 1637. Ferdinand III was basically a peace loving person. Soon after he assumed the imperial throne, he embarked on an effort to forge peace treaties with both France

---

[9] See A. Levi, *Cardinal Richelieu and the Making of France*, NY: Carroll & Graf Publishers (2000); D. Parrott, *Richelieu's Army: War, Government, and Society in France, 1624-1642*, CUP (2001); J. Pietkiewicz, *My Kingdom for a Valley: The Valtelline Episode and Richelieu's Raison d'Etat*, M.A. Thesis, Youngstown State University (2004); Spiteri, *At Your Fingertips* III, n. 20 (a).

[10] See G. Treasure, *Mazarin: The Crisis of Absolutism in France*, NY (1995); Spiteri, *At Your Fingertips* III, n. 20 (b).

and Sweden. Furthermore, in 1644, he conceded to all German States the possibility to conduct their own respective foreign policy, whether it was for peace or to continue the bloodshed of the Thirty Years War. The edict provided another incentive for his brother-in-law, Philip IV of Spain, to block the election of a pro-French Pope during the conclave of 1644.

By the time Philip IV of Spain died in 1665, the Spanish Empire had reached its zenith but its vastness, coupled with political and military corruption and adversity, was also the roots of its own undoing. As a young teen-age King, he allowed himself to be guided by very capable men. His favorite was Gaspar de Guzmán y Acevedo, 1st Count-Duke of Olivares.[11] He controlled Spain's domestic and foreign policies until his downfall in 1643.

Unfortunately, Philip IV's political opinions were identical to those of his father, Philip III, and his grandfather, Philip II. He was convinced that it was his duty to support his Hapsburg relative, the Emperor. Thus, Spain was in a constant, exorbitant and very exhausting state of war with Protestant princes, the Dutch, France, and England. In the same grain as his father and grandfather and great-grandfather, Emperor Charles V, he viewed his reign in terms of God entrusting to him the cause of the Catholic Church, despite his debauched private life and a warped perception of what the Church and the Papacy were all about. His reign turned out to be one of the most inept in Europe. He entered the Thirty Years War to assist his cousin Ferdinand III, despite the fact that his wife was the French King's sister and the French Queen was his own sister.[12]

---

[11] See J.H. Elliot, *The Count-Duke of Olivares: The Statesman in an Age of Decline*, New Haven: YUP (1986).

[12] Elisabeth of France was the first wife of Philip IV and Queen Consort of Spain from 1621 to 1644. On the other hand, Anne of Austria was the wife of Louis

Philip IV's ministers thought it was imperative that the successor to Urban VIII be pro-Hapsburg. Consequently, Cardinal Gil Carrillo de Albornoz launched the first ever veto[13] against the *papabile*, Cardinal Giulio Cesare Sacchetti, a former Papal Nuncio to Spain. The Cardinal had been too closely associated with Urban VIII and his pro-French policies. Cardinal Giambattista Pamphilj had replaced Sacchetti as Papal Nuncio to Spain. Ironically, Pamphilj was also a former Papal Nuncio to France and Mazarin rushed to the conclave to declare a veto against his candidacy, arriving too late because Pamphilj had already been elected as Innocent X.[14] The conclave had proven to be a very stormy one, marred with outside secular interference through Cardinal-Electors who carried with them the interests of France and the Hapsburgs respectively.

## 53. Continued Secular Interference in Papal Elections

The character of the composition of the College of Cardinals radically changed over the centuries.[15] On the eve of the Renaissance, the body began to be infiltrated with private and hidden agendas that belonged more to the secular rather than to the spiritual sphere. Outside interference by secular potentates became gradually so pronounced and controlling during conclaves that it was not unusual for them to last weeks or even months, pestered with factional intrigues and bickering. Crown-Cardinals carried

---

XIII and Queen Consort of France and Navarre upon marrying Louis XIII in 1615.

[13] It is of some interest to note that the first and the last vetoes in papal elections were posited by the Hapsburgs, the first by the Spanish branch and the last by the Austrian branch.

[14] See Spiteri *At Your Fingertips* III, n. 19 (e).

[15] See Spiteri, *The Emerging Role of the Cardinals and Papal Elections*, op. cit.

the veto of their respective secular masters and used it to block a specific *papabile*. There were instances when some Cardinals voted for papal candidates as a sign of their opposition to the dead Pontiff's policies. It can be stated by a person of faith that the Holy Spirit, who consistently guides and protects the Catholic Church, works with what people present to Him rather than with what He prefers!

Nineteen Popes were elected during the period being covered in this volume. Many of the conclaves that assembled to elect these Popes were marred with political intrigues and vetoes. This proved very detrimental to the Universal Church. A candidate usually ended up being elected as a result of a compromise. This said, it should be recalled that many Popes did not follow through with the political agendas of their electors.

The intrigues involved in the election of Innocent X have been presented above. Alexander VII was elected Pope in April 1655 after an eighty-day conclave that was prolonged mainly by Cardinal Mazarin, who had France's interests at heart, and by Spain's renewed veto against Cardinal Sacchetti. The conclave concluded only after Cardinal Mazarin resentfully withdrew France's veto. Clement IX was elected Pope in June 1667 at the end of an eighteen-day conclave. The candidate had entered the conclave with the support of both the kings of France and Spain. Clement X was elected in April 1670 after an almost five-month long conclave, during which time some Cardinals entered and exited and then re-entered the conclave, while others later joined the conclave, still others got sick during the conclave and had to leave. France and Spain used their veto power against a number of *papabili*.[16] Blessed Innocent XI was elected in September 1676

---

[16] France vetoed Cardinal Benedetto Odescalchi and Spain vetoed Cardinals Pietro Vidoni and Francesco Maria Brancaccio.

after a two-month conclave once France agreed to withhold its veto against this *papabile*. France had already posted a veto against him in the previous conclave. Alexander VIII was elected in October 1689 after an almost six-week conclave, having overcome Louis XIV's concerns about his future relations with France. Spain had vetoed Cardinal Lorenzo Brancati di Lauria. Innocent XII was elected in July 1691, after a five-month conclave that was prolonged by conflicts between pro-French and pro-Imperial Cardinal-Electors.

The eighteenth century also witnessed secular vetoes during conclaves. Clement XI was elected in November 1700 at the end of a forty-five day conclave. The prolongation of the conclave was due to the bickering between the French and Imperial factions, with France vetoing Cardinal Galeazzo Marescotti. In the end, the day was won by those Cardinals who wanted a Pope who was primarily concerned with the inner life of the Church. Innocent XIII was elected in May 1721 after a five-week conclave, during which Austria vetoed Cardinal Fabrizio Paolucci and Spain vetoed Cardinal Francesco Pignatelli. Benedict XIII was elected in May 1724 after a nine-week conclave that was marred with dissent among the Cardinals from France, Spain, and Austria.[17] Clement XII was elected in July 1730 after a four-month very stormy conclave. Spain vetoed Cardinals Giuseppe Renato Imperiali and Antonfelice Zondadari. About half of the fifty-four Cardinal-Electors had been presented as candidates at one stage or another! Benedict XIV was elected in August 1740 after a six-month conclave. His election was a last minute compromise which took the Cardinals by surprise. Spain vetoed Cardinal Pier

---

[17] The new Pope initially called himself Benedict XIV but soon changed his numerical title to XIII since the person who had that name before was the infamous anti-pope Pedro de Luna. See Spiteri, *At Your Fingertips* I, n. 61 (b).

Marcelino Corradini. Clement XIII was elected in July 1758 after an almost four-month long conclave during which time France originally vetoed his possible election as well as vetoed Cardinal Carlo Alberto Guidobono Cavalchini. The majority of the Cardinal-Electors chose him as a reaction to the pontificate of Benedict XIV. Clement XIV was elected in May 1769 during a very contested three-month conclave. For the first time in a number of centuries, all Cardinal-Electors participated in a conclave and not one of them died during its sitting. The entire conclave was marred with sheer political intrigues of Cardinals who pushed the secular agenda of their respective sovereigns, particularly Spain's insistence on the suppression of the Jesuits. Pius VI was elected in February 1775 after an almost four-and-one-half month conclave. Spain, France, and the Kingdom of the Two Sicilies had vetoed Cardinal Giovanni Carlo Boschi.

The three-and-one-half month conclave which ushered in the nineteenth century was held in Venice, under the protection of Emperor Francis II who also presented his veto against Cardinals Hyacinthe Sigismond Gerdil and Carlo Bellisomi. Cardinal Gregorio Barnaba Chiaramonti was elected as Pius VII in March 1800. During this Pontificate, Holy Roman Emperor Francis II became Emperor Francis I of Austria when the Holy Roman Empire was abolished in 1806. Austria maintained all of the imperial privileges granted by the Holy See.

Two pronouncedly opposed groups emerged during the papacy of Pius VII: the *zelanti* and the *politicani*. Both had their own idea of how the Church should be run. The *zelanti* wanted a highly centralized Church and were strongly opposed to any secularization reforms that were slowly creeping into the Papal States and the Roman Curia. The *politicani*, though not liberal, were a rather moderate faction who wanted the Church to deal with problems which new ideologies and the Industrial Revolution were heralding into society at large. Secretary of State, Cardinal Consalvi was perceived as their leader. The group was against the isolation of the Papacy. Austria and France, in particular, also wanted to make sure that the Cardinal-Electors did not elect a Pope with what they considered to be fanatical tendencies. But the Catholic European Crowns could not agree among themselves as how to proceed.

Apart from secular rulers interfering through a veto during a conclave, it was also customary for their ambassadors to say a few words to the Cardinal-Electors before their sequestration. These speeches usually fell on deaf ears either because the speakers were not understood or some Cardinals were already exasperated or bored. The 1823 conclave turned out to be one full of political intrigue and manipulation. Austria vetoed Cardinal Giuseppe Albani. Cardinal Annibale della Genga was elected as Leo XII in September.

It took eighty-three voting sessions to elect Gregory XVI as Pope in February 1831. Spain vetoed Cardinal Giacomo Giustiniani. On the other hand, Cardinal Giovanni Maria Mastai Ferretti was elected as (Blessed) Pius IX in June 1846, during a two-day conclave. The veto of Austria against him arrived too late to influence the conclave. And lastly, Austria vetoed Cardinal Mariano Rampolla during the conclave of 1903. The conclave elected Cardinal Giuseppe Sarto as (St.) Pius X in June 1903. This Pope gave a deadly blow to the veto powers of all secular authorities in 1904. There has never been such a veto since.

# CHAPTER SEVENTEEN

# The Popes and Rome

## 54. The Baroque

Protestant reformers of the sixteenth and seventeenth centuries can be caricatured as belligerent, dour, cynical, iconoclastic, and distrustful of any authority except that of Sacred Scriptures. The enforcement of the Protestant Reformation in central and northern Europe had been drenched with violence.

The term *barocco* was first used to suggest disapproval. The term is thought to derive from a Portuguese word for a misshapen pearl. Certainly unbalance and excess are the qualities which Baroque artists indulged in and turned to advantage. No matter how it is sliced, the Catholic world is the natural home of the Baroque. Its mood suits the message of the Catholic Counter-Reformation. The mood of the Baroque is very different from the dignified and often severe masterpieces of the Renaissance.[1]

The Catholic Church has been the greatest patron of the arts for many centuries. One has to simply recall, for example, the Renaissance Movement. She had long used art and music

---

[1] See M. Levey, *Painting in 18th Century Venice*, Ithaca, NY: Cornell University Press (1980); M. Stokstad (ed.), *Art History*, 3rd ed., NJ: Prentice-Hall (2005); M. Bussagli, M. Reiche, *Baroque and Rococo*, Sterling Publishing Co. (2009); L.H. Zirpolo, *Historical Dictionary of Baroque Art and Architecture*, Scarecrow Press (2010).

with great skill to touch the emotions of her faithful. Following the Protestant Reformation, the time was ripe for the Church to appeal once again to the emotions and senses of her members and those who visited her churches. Thus, the Catholic Counter-Reformation developed the Baroque style for religious purposes and as part of the Church's program to instruct the common believer in matters of Catholic doctrine and to emotionally and visually appeal to her members. The Baroque, realistic and illusionist and personal and intensely dramatic, was born in Italy, and later adopted, with varying degrees, in France, Germany, Austria, Netherlands, Spain, Portugal, and Malta.

Originally the Baroque was primarily associated with the religious tensions between Roman Catholicism and Protestantism. The Catholic European countries of the seventeenth and eighteenth centuries saw the expansion of the Baroque style in paintings, sculpture and architecture. These three arts were combined inside many churches and chapels where, soon enough, people could also contemplate the beauty found within and pray while listening to Baroque music. This was in stark contrast to many of the Protestant faiths in that many were iconoclastic in their attitude, lacked the celebration of Mass, and focused mainly on preaching based on Sacred Scripture.

The Flemish devout Catholic Peter Paul Rubens, along with some others, is considered as the main representative of the Baroque style in art. His lively paintings emphasized movement, color, and sensuality. Furthermore, he was a classically-educated humanist scholar, art collector, and diplomat. He is famous for his Counter-Reformation altarpieces, portraits, landscapes, hunt scenes, and paintings of mythological and allegorical subjects. Rubens later became one of the leading voices of the Catholic Counter-Reformation style of painting. In due time, the style made some inroads into Protestant countries. For instance, the Flemish Baroque style was developed to emphasize realism of everyday life. Dutch geniuses like Rembrandt van Rijn and Jan Vermeer, its superlative proponents, utilized the Baroque style of painting for religious and secular settings, but not as a response to the directives of the Catholic Counter-Reformation.

The Italian Giovanni Lorenzo Bernini[2] transformed Rome into a Baroque city. He left his lasting mark inside St. Peter's Basilica and around St. Peter's Square with his famous colonnades and the balustrade above the columns where a series of saints seem to be speaking with one another of the center figure, the Risen Christ. Bernini was appointed architect of St. Peter's Basilica in 1629, three years after its dedication. The new Basilica bestowed a new dignity to the ancient city. Bernini, for the next forty years, was determined to leave his perennial mark on both the Basilica and the city. Thus, he gradually provided magnificent features which impressed arriving pilgrims and continue to do so down to our own days.

Numerous churches during the seventeenth century were either built or decorated in the Baroque style. Following the example of the new St. Peter's in Rome, they put the Baroque at the service of the Church's message. The faithful are welcomed by rows of saints, gesticulating eagerly in stone from alcove or roof line. Inside a Baroque church, light falls on mingling curves of columns and altars and sculpted groups, breaking up the solidity of side walls and often leading the eye up to an illusionist ceiling on which angels and saints stream upwards into the distant clouds of heaven. There is nothing half-hearted about Baroque until the subtle hesitation in the eighteenth century which produced the Rococo.

---

[2] See Spiteri, *At Your Fingertips* III, n. 23 (b).

Catholic people could contemplate and pray in church while listening to Baroque music. Yet, some of the greatest Baroque music composers were Protestant, such as Georg Frederick Handel, Johann Sebastian Bach, Johann Georg Pisendel, Gottfried Heinrich Stölzel, Henry Purcell, and Georg Philipp Telemann. Catholic composers included such giants as Arcangelo Corelli, Francesco Geminiani, Nicola Porpura, Alessandro Scarlatti and his son Domenico, Pietro Francesco Cavalli, Francesco Durante, Giovanni Batista Pergolesi, Antonio Vivaldi, Giovanni Battista Lulli, Francois Couperin.

Secular governments also adopted the Baroque style, but their intention was for monarchical self-aggrandizement. However, it should be remembered that while the Catholic Church used the Baroque style for religious reasons, secular governments used it for a manifestation of political power.

## 55. The Rococo

*Rococo* is a term which refers to the "Late Baroque" style of the eighteenth century which began in France. The term is a combination of two French words: "rocaille" meaning stone, and "coquilles" meaning shell. These two objects served as motifs of decoration. Today, Rococo is widely recognized as a major period in the development of European art.

Rococo emerged from the decorative arts and interior design, moving from architecture and furniture to sculpture and painting. Rich Baroque designs started being replaced with lighter elements with more curves and natural patterns during the reign of Louis XV, reflecting the current French excesses. Though the Rococo still maintained the Baroque complex forms and intricate patterns, it began to add a variety of diverse characteristics, including a taste for Oriental designs and asymmetric compositions.

The Rococo style spread with French artists and engraved publications. It was readily received in the Catholic parts of Germany, Bohemia, and Austria, where it was merged with German Baroque traditions. It is found in churches and palaces, particularly in the south. Architects often draped their interiors with clouds of fluffy white stucco. In Italy, the late Baroque styles of Borromini and Guarini set the tone for Rococo in Turin, Venice, Naples, and Sicily. However, Rome and Tuscany persevered in their preference of Baroque. Contemporary Britain did not accept Rococo architecture, though its influence can be seen in British silverware, porcelain, silk, and furniture. The French Enlightenment frequently criticized Rococo for its superficiality. France abandoned Rococo on the eve of the French Revolution. Germany saw Rococo as being outlandish by the late eighteenth century. However, Britain developed a taste for Rococo in the middle of the nineteenth century. Generally speaking, however, the Catholic Church deemed Rococo as a perversion of Baroque. The latter was adopted by the Church so as to elevate one's mind to higher things. Rococo was perceived as producing the opposite effect and as a source of major distraction to a person who wants to encounter the Lord in church. It was argued that Rococo defeated the purpose for going to church and was unsuitable for church settings.

## 56. Popes as Patrons of the Arts

By the time of the celebration of the Jubilee Year 1650, Rome had become transformed by the genius of Bernini and had become the master of the Baroque. This is essentially the Rome which visitors see today.

Alexander VIII bought the entire library of Queen Christina of Sweden in 1689 and donated it to the Vatican Apostolic Library. By being brought over to Rome, the library was spared going up in flames with the entire royal palace in Stockholm in 1697.

Much of Rome suffered devastation with a major earthquake in 1703. Part of the Coliseum collapsed. There was much restoration to be done. The long pontificate of Clement XI, a patron of the arts, allowed him to follow through many of his restoration plans, despite the fact that the Papal States were in a deep financial crisis. He had a famous sundial added in the Church of Santa Maria degli Angeli e dei Martiri, an obelisk erected on the fountain in Piazza della Rotonda, and a river port built on the Tiber River. He provided the statuary around St. Peter's Square and made extensive restorations to several prominent churches in Rome. He established a committee, under Carlo Maratta and Carlo Fontana, to complete the statuary decorations of St. John Lateran. He erected a statue of Charlemagne opposite Bernini's Constantine. Moreover, he founded a painting and sculpting academy in the Campidoglio. He enriched the Vatican Apostolic Library with many Oriental codices. Being an archaeological dilettante, he financed the first archaeological excavations in the Roman catacombs, passed stringent laws to protect the cultural heritage of Rome, and asked the architect and engraver Alessandro Specchi to compile a catalog of ancient buildings and works of art in 1714. On the other hand, Benedict XIII inaugurated the famous Spanish Steps in 1727 and founded the University of Camerino.

Clement XII built the new façade of the papal cathedral, St. John Lateran. He also began the construction of the famous

Trevi Fountain, paved the streets of Rome and its environs, and bought Cardinal Alessandro Albani's collection of antiquities for the papal gallery on the Capitol. He enriched the Vatican Apostolic Library and sent Joseph Simeon Assemani to the East in search of manuscripts. He also restored the Arch of Constantine and built the palace of the Consulta on the Quirinal. Moreover, he had the Ancona port constructed and drained the malarial marshes of the Chiana near Lake Trasimeno.

Benedict XIV, probably the most prolific papal scholar since the Middle Ages, founded four academies at Rome. These were that for the study of Roman antiquities, the study of Christian antiquities, the study of the history of the Church and the councils, and finally, the history of Canon Law and liturgy. He established a Christian museum, and commissioned Joseph Assemani to prepare a catalogue of the manuscripts in the Vatican Apostolic Library, which he enriched by purchasing and donating the Ottobonian Library that had 3,300 manuscripts of unique value and importance. He founded chairs of chemistry and mathematics in the Roman University of the Sapienza. Other schools were funded for chairs in painting and sculpture. He commissioned many projects for the building and adornment of churches in Rome, including providing money for the completion of the Trevi Fountain in 1742. He was far from threatened with the Enlightenment and corresponded with some of its prominent leaders.

Clement XIII had the nude classical statues in the Vatican provided with fig leaves! Nonetheless, he tried to restore some artistic magnificence to Rome but at the cost of his impoverished subjects. Pius VI followed up on the idea of his predecessor and established the Vatican Museums as an independent entity from the Vatican Apostolic Library and completed the Pio-Clementino Museum. The marshy lands near Città della Pieve, Perugia, Spo-

leto, and Trevi were drained during his pontificate. He unsuccessfully tried to do the same with the Pontine Marshes. The latter
were finally drained in the late 1930s under the Fascist dictator
Benito Mussolini.

Pius VII began a systematic approach towards the restoration and upkeep of the ancient Roman monuments. This major
undertaking involved Trajan's Forum, the Coliseum, Via Appia
Antica, and the Arch of Titus. One of the outstanding persons
the Pope enlisted was Antonio Canova. The Pope and prominent
wealthy Roman families tried their best, but with limited success,
to regain the objects of art that had left the Papal States in previous years or had been carried away to Paris by Napoleon. The
Pope also expanded the Pio-Clementino Museum, adding to it
the Chiaramonti Museum, the Braccio Nuovo and the Lapidary
Gallery. He directed that Galileo's works were removed from
the Index. The Holy Office, at his behest in 1822, granted an
imprimatur to the work of Settele, in which heliocentricism was
presented as a physical fact and no longer as an hypothesis.

Gregory XVI founded the Etruscan and Egyptian Museums at the Vatican, and the Christian Museum at the Lateran.
He lavished aid to rebuild the burnt down St. Paul-Outside-the-
Walls and encouraged archeological study of the Roman Forum
and the catacombs.

## 57. Jewish Relations

There was a place in Rome known as the Roman Ghetto, but
more popularly called the Jewish Ghetto. It was a walled quarter
with three gates. It was located in the rione Sant'Angelo. Paul IV
set apart the Jews in Rome in 1555 by papal decree. Up till then,

Jews had lived freely in Rome since ancient times. The papal decree was harsh and anti-Jewish in its measures. It segregated Jews from the much larger Catholic community, had the Ghetto's gates locked every night, rendered Jews as second-class citizens, and required them to listen to sermons every Sabbath. They also had to petition annually for permission to live there, could not own any property in any part of the Papal States, had to pay a yearly tax for living in the Ghetto, and had to swear loyalty to the Pope each year. These conditions, except for a very brief period, remained in effect until 1848. Some Jews, however, welcomed the isolation of the Ghetto, arguing it protected their small community from possible attacks by Catholics, preserved their Jewish identity from outside interference, and discouraged insecure Jews from assimilating into the larger Catholic community.[3]

The dreaded Portuguese Inquisition[4] was, for all effects, a civil branch of the Portuguese government. Even so, Clement X, in defense of the Marranos, suspended the Portuguese Inquisition's activities against them in 1674. Since the papal suspension went unheeded, Blessed Innocent XI suspended the grand inquisitor in 1679. This Pope had a limited pro-Jewish policy. He compelled Venice to release all Jewish prisoners and discouraged compulsory baptism of Jews, though he failed to eradicate this shameful practice. However, after the Papal Edict was postponed two times, he decreed in October 1682 that all the money-lending activities carried out by the Roman Jews were to cease.

An interesting papal decision took place in February 1747 in that Benedict XIV confirmed a decision the Roman Curia had taken one hundred and fifty years earlier (1597), which stated that

---

[3] See O. Chadwick, *A History of the Popes 1830-1914*, OUP (1998).
[4] See Spiteri, *At Your Fingertips* III, n. 14.

a Jewish child, once baptized, even when done against Church law, must be brought up as a Catholic. But he forbade the forceful baptism of adult Jews and declared that such acts are invalid. When Jews began being persecuted in Poland, he denounced the act and joined the Primate of Poland to defend the victims. He instructed Cardinal Ganganelli, the future Clement XIV, to investigate the blood accusation against Jews in Yanopol, which was judged unfounded. Once Ganganelli became Pope, he immediately removed the Jews from the jurisdiction of the Roman Inquisition and placed them directly under that of the Vicariate of Rome.

The Ghetto was legally abolished during the short-lived Roman Republic which was instituted by the French in 1798. But the Ghetto and the pre-republic conditions were reinstated after the Pope regained control of Rome.

Leo XII had a manifest anti-Jewish policy. He passed laws forbidding Jews to own property, giving them the shortest possible time to sell it. He revived a defunct Middle Ages practice that required Jews to be segregated and to wear a humiliating mark on their clothing, and placed them back under the Roman Inquisition. Moreover, he insisted that all Roman residents, including Jews, must listen to commentaries on the Catholic catechism each week. His repressive policies forced many Jews to leave Rome for northern Italy.

Blessed Pius IX ordered the demolition of the Ghetto walls in 1848. However, due to a great resistance from the Romans, the task was carried out during the night. But it was not until September 1870 that Jews in Rome ceased to be considered second-class citizens.

# The Glory of the Catholic Church

# CHAPTER EIGHTEEN

# Missionary Activities

The greatest treasure and gift that the Catholic Church has is Jesus Christ. Her glory lies in the fact of bringing the Lord's Good News to all nations and making Him ever-present among His people through the sacraments, particularly the Eucharist. The missionary activities of the Church, despite their hardships and travails, form part of her glory. On the other hand, her Saints and Blesseds are the stars that shine, reminding us mortals that everything is possible with God. They are our brothers and sisters, and our heroes.

The years of Church history being surveyed in this volume are full of missionary activity amidst success, maltreatment, and social and political turmoil. They are also full of numerous Catholics who laid down their life for their Catholic Faith and who were joined with many others who spent their lives for love of God and neighbor in the midst of humiliations, persecution, martyrdom, much unrest, and wars.

## 58. Missions in the Seventeenth Century

(a) The seventeenth century witnessed a gigantic missionary activity of the Church throughout the world. The impetus in Asia had been supplied by St. Francis Xavier in the sixteenth century. His endeavor was followed by many fellow Jesuits and other religious communities, especially the Capuchins and the Dominicans, not only in Asia, but also in the New World, in Africa, and even in Europe itself. Nonetheless, Popes were not spared internal and external political intrigues while the missionary activities of her members were being carried out. Some of these issues were the result of a clash between the Western culture and the diverse and respective native cultures in the missions. Others resulted from political decisions taken by respective European Catholic Crowns who were also masters of specific overseas colonies. Also, some papal decisions helped the missions while others were detrimental and had long-lasting effects.

Innocent X, in 1645, raised the Colegio de Santo Tomas de la Nuestra Señora del Santissimo Rosario in Manila, the Philippines, to the University of Santo Tomas. It became the oldest and still existing University in all of Asia. It was originally founded by missionaries and the Dominicans remain in charge of it. The Philippines at the time was a Spanish possession.

Clement X recognized the apostolic endeavors of the French missionaries in Canada, then called New France, and established the diocese of Quebec in 1674. It was the first Catholic diocese north of Mexico. He also declared the first American saint, Rose of Lima, in 1671.

Although a number of Popes had addressed the issue of what came to be called the "Chinese Rites Controversy," the problem lingered on because each religious community which was not pleased with a papal decision simply waited for a new Pope and then appealed. In essence, the issue regarded the promotion by Jesuit missionaries of the Chinese custom of ancestor worship and the inculturation of the Catholic Faith. Clement XI forbade

Jesuit missionaries to promote such practices. Innocent XIII did the same and also suspended the recruitment of new members to the Society of Jesus. Subsequently, in the Papal Bulls *Ex quo singulari* of 1742 and *Omnium sollicitudinum* of 1744, Benedict XIV rebuked the missionary methods of the Jesuits in accommodating Catholic teachings to the heathen usages of the Chinese and of the natives of Malabar. He terminated the catechetical and liturgical approaches in China.[1] As a result, the Catholic Church in China began undergoing persecution. However, he allowed some accommodation to the Indian culture in the Malabar Rite.

Pius VI gave the United States its first diocese. He established the See of Baltimore, Maryland, in 1789 in response to the request made by the clergy in the United States in March 1788.

(b) Benedict XIV had granted the right of Padroado to João V of Portugal in 1740 for all the dioceses and abbeys in Portugal and its vast empire. The following year, the Pope issued the Papal Bull, *Immensa pastorum principis*, demanding more humane treatment for the Indians of Brazil and Paraguay and denouncing the dissolution of reducciones in Paraguay. Nonetheless, he granted the title of "Most Faithful Majesty" to the king in 1748.

Prime Minister Pombal of Portugal was determined to suppress the Jesuits. He perceived them as standing in his way to power and liberal thought. The papal demands and criticism of Portugal in 1741 brewed in the background. The Jesuit experiment of reducciones had become too successful and too independent for the Portuguese Crown. An opportunity arose when the Indios rebelled because they had been ordered to abandon their respective reducciones and relocate to the forests, which meant

---

[1]  See J. Gernet, *China and the Christian Impact: A Conflict of Cultures* (J. Lloyd, trans.), U.K.: CUP (1985); S. Whalley Jr., X. Wu (gen. eds.), *China and Christianity: Burdened Past, Hopeful Future*, San Francisco: East Gate Books (2000).

losing their homes and possessions. Pombal accused the Jesuits of instigating the rebellion. A second and more serious opportunity arose when a slighted member of the Tovara family made an attempt on the life of the king in September 1758. Pombal declared the entire Tovara family guilty of attempted regicide, accused the Jesuits of being accomplice, imprisoned all of them, and confiscated their possessions. He then asked Clement XIII to allow him to punish them. When the Pope advised Pombal to give them a fair trial, the Prime Minister felt slighted, kept the Jesuit superiors imprisoned and shipped the rest to Civitavecchia. Two years later, Pombal allowed a smearing campaign through the publication of a number of pamphlets, the most injurious being "the Brief Relation," which subversively portrayed the Jesuits as having set up their virtual kingdom in South America while terrorizing the Indios.[2]

On the other hand, Spain was also given a limited red carpet treatment. The Spanish Crown was allowed to tax Church revenues and clergy benefices in 1741. The Spanish Padronado was extended in 1753 to almost all nominations to Church benefices within the realm. The next year, an agreement was reached with Rome wherein Church revenues in Spain and its vast American colonies were diverted to the Spanish treasury so as to assist that kingdom's war against African pirates.

(c) Some of the Church's missionary activities in Southern Asia did not go well, as had been the case with China. This was particularly true in Sri Lanka (Ceylon). King Rājasimha II of Kandy asked the Calvinist Dutch East India Company to help him get rid of the Portuguese from his kingdom. After over two

---

[2]  See A. Greer, (ed.), *The Jesuit Relations: Natives and Missionaries in 17th Century North America*, NY: Bedford/St. Martin's Press (2000); J. Martinez, *Not Counting the Cost: Jesuit Missionaries in Colonial Mexico*, Loyola Press (2001); O.E. Gonzalez, J.L. Gonzalez, *Christianity in Latin America: A History*, CUP (2008).

decades of fighting, the Portuguese capitulated in Colombo and Jaffna, in 1656 and 1658 respectively. However, by then the Catholic presence in the kingdom had taken root. The king realized too late that he had exchanged one set of masters with another.

The Calvinist Dutch took measures to stamp out Catholicism from the entire island, fearing the disloyalty of Catholics and the return of the Portuguese. The Catholic Faith was banned, churches and schools were confiscated, and all priests were banished. Persons caught giving shelter or assisting any priest could be executed. Moreover, Catholics were required to attend Dutch Calvinist services, to baptize their children Calvinist, to marry in the Calvinist Kirk, and to be buried according to Calvinist rites. Blessed Innocent XI, once aware of the situation, fruitlessly attempted through the Propagation of the Faith to induce Leopold I of Austria and Bishop Johannes Baptista van Neercassel, Vicar Apostolic to the Netherlands, to prevail upon the Dutch government and allow a handful of Catholic priests to go to Sri Lanka. However, an Indian Oratorian priest from Goa, (Blessed) Joseph Vaz, managed to sneak on the island in 1687. His missionary activities, which included spending a stint in prison, ended with his death in 1711. He had been in time allowed to minister to the Catholic community and was appointed Vicar General for the island in 1696. By this time other missionaries of Indian origin began to arrive to assist him. However, the Catholic Church was to experience more persecution on the island.

(d) The French government began to realize the potential value of the natural and commercial resources of its vast possessions in New France. At the time France did not interfere with the natives' way of life or impose French laws or customs. Locals primarily perceived the French as allies and customers for their furs.

But France's claim to this territory was contested by the English due to the affluent fur trade. It was a matter of time before local clashes escalated into war. Though the English eventually gained full dominion over what is today called Canada, there remains a profound French influence and an ongoing tension between the English-speaking and French-speaking Canadians.

The French program to build forts and set up settlements in New France was very expensive. The funds came from commercial colonizers who sought to monopolize the extremely profitable fur trade industry in North America. Pierre du Gua de Monts, founder of the earliest permanent French settlement in North America, acquired such a monopoly from Louis XIV of France. He established a post in Acadia in 1604. Then, Samuel de Champlain established a settlement at Québec on the St. Lawrence River in 1608 and eventually convinced Cardinal Richelieu of the importance of France's new territory. He had realized that the inland fur trade could be easily monopolized and better protected by settling on land where the banks of the St. Lawrence were narrow rather than in places on the open coast of Acadia. Consequently, French colonies began to focus on the St. Lawrence valley. The Cardinal organized the Company of One Hundred Associates to develop and administer New France in 1627.

De Champlain entered into alliances with the local Algonquian nations and their inland allies, the Huron Confederacy, so that they would provide fur for him at Québec and he could travel long distances unharmed as he furthered his business and mapped out northeastern North America from Newfoundland to the Great Lakes. The French colony continued to prosper after his death. A new French settlement was established at Montréal in 1642, though it remained small in population and mostly dependent on the fur trade.

After the French failed to aid the Huron Confederacy in a war with the Iroquois during the 1640's, from which the former emerged victorious in 1649, the fur trade was temporarily devastated until a number of Algonquian nations replaced the Huron as French allies and suppliers. Next, the French undertook more explorations. Then, in 1663, Louis XIV's finance minister, Jean-Baptiste Colbert, abolished the One Hundred Associates and declared New France as a royal province to be ruled from Québec by a governor-general and an advisory Superior Council. The defenses were improved, a campaign against the Iroquois in 1665 led to a peace treaty, more soldiers were sent, and the French Crown subsidized immigration, including that of clergy and religious, to the newest royal province.

England challenged France in the fur trade after 1670 and a number of wars took place before New France completely fell to British dominance.[3] Charles II of England had granted a trade monopoly in the area of Hudson Bay to a London group, the Hudson's Bay Company. Competition was fierce, but the French combined the fur trade with exploration and missionary work. Louis Joliet and the Jesuit Jacques Marquette began exploring the Mississippi River in 1673. Robert de la Salle reached the Gulf of Mexico in 1682.

The Catholic Church had a powerful presence in French colonial society. French Protestants were restricted from going to New France. Catholic religious communities were entrusted with maintaining and spreading the Catholic Faith. The first to arrive, in 1615, were the Franciscan Recollects who were followed and practically replaced by the Jesuits in 1633. The Ursuline

---

[3] The two major wars were King William's War, during which time the Iroquois sided with the British, and Queen Anne's War. There were also many battles fought between the French and the native Indians during this time.

nuns, dedicated to teaching girls, arrived in 1639 and the Sulpician priests, who ran seminaries, arrived in 1657. Gradually, the Church became more and more established in New France and members from the local communities became Catholic.

The great missionary Blessed François-Xavier de Montmorency-Laval[4] was the first Roman Catholic bishop in New France. He was one of the most influential men of his day, founding many churches and institutes of learning, including seminaries. He believed that the local Church should have priests who were trained locally. He got religious communities to run hospitals and schools, and stabilized their existence through owning estates under the seigniorial system, thereby making them big landlords.

---

## 59. Missions in the Eighteenth Century

(a) The eighteenth century was a tragic century for the Catholic Church. There was a pronounced and significant decline in her spiritual and political influence, as she experienced setbacks and reversals. The staunch Catholic empires of Spain and Portugal, which had assisted in the spreading of the Catholic Faith, collapsed as world powers and were replaced by Protestant powers, particularly England and Holland. The Japanese and Chinese empires continued to persecute Catholics. Catholic missionaries were expelled or executed, and local Catholic communities were severely persecuted and, at times, martyred. The Catholic Japanese community went underground for two centuries.

---

4   Bishop Laval, a nobleman, was appointed Vicar Apostolic of New France and ordained as Titular Bishop of Petra, Palestine, in 1658. He became the first Bishop of Québec in 1674 and resigned the See in 1688. John Paul II declared Bishop Laval as "Blessed" on 22nd June 1980.

The Catholic missionary activities, with the greatest exception of the Philippines, were practically stopped in the Far East. On the other hand, the Papal dissolution of the Society of Jesus in 1773 did not help matters in the least. The Jesuits had become the foremost cultural organizers and one of the strongest economic and political forces in the entire Spanish and Portuguese world. They had supplied thousands of missionaries who eventually began to defend the Indios against the brutally abusive colonial powers. Their superb educational programs and missionary activities came to a complete halt. Moreover, the ancient power of the Catholic Church in France was destroyed by the outbreak and aftermath of the French Revolution and the rising of Napoleon. At the same time, while the spiritual and political influence of the Church was declining, there was an evangelical revival of the various Protestant denominations in northern Europe and the United States.

(b) There emerged a note of hope in Sri Lanka. Sri Vijaya Rājasimha was not a native by birth. Upon assuming the throne, he needed the support of the local islanders and the Dutch to survive. Some local Buddhists and their monks, along with the Dutch, did not want a Catholic presence in Kandy. Consequently, a new wave of persecutions ensued. After several Catholic priests had been arrested and tried, the king, in 1746, banished them from his kingdom. The missionaries found refuge in the Vanni from where missionaries secretly ministered to Catholics in both the kingdom of Kandy and the Dutch domains.

The tide turned toward Catholics when war broke out in 1762 between the King of Kandy and the Dutch. The Catholics sided with the Dutch. The latter, as a gesture of appreciation, allowed Catholic priests to minister to their flock under restricted conditions, though the anti-Catholic laws were not abolished.

## 60. Missions in the Americas

(a) Yet, the eighteenth century was not completely full of gloom and doom for the Catholic Church. Blessed Fray Junípero Serra[5] is known today as the "Apostle of the Californias" and his statue stands in the Capitol Rotunda in Washington, D.C.[6] He was born as Miguel Serra y Abram in Petra in 1713 on the island of Majorca. He joined the Franciscans at age sixteen, taking the religious name of Junípero. Having excelled in school, he volunteered for the missions in the Spanish New World in 1749. By this time, the Spanish culture and Catholic religious influence were amply manifest in the urban centers. The unexplored areas were regarded as mission territory.

Serra's first assignment was to the mountainous region of Sierra Gorda, where he preached to the Indios. His next assignment was to the Indios living on the coastal villages and in mining camps. Despite his chronically infected and ulcerated leg, he walked over 6,000 miles on foot, preaching and administering the sacraments. After Spain banished the Jesuits from its dominions in 1767, the thirteen Jesuit missions in Baja California were suddenly left unstaffed. Serra was appointed the new Superior of Baja California. In a matter of a few years, he was sent to Alta California where, in 1769, he was named Padre Presidente of California. He immediately became the founder of a string of missions in that vast territory, beginning with San Diego. Of the twenty-one missions set up along the coast of California, he

---

[5] Pope John Paul II declared Fray Junípero Serra as "Blessed" on 25th September 1988.

[6] See M.N.L. Couve de Murville, *The Man Who Founded California: The Life of Blessed Junipero Serra*, Ignatius Press (2000); Eberhardt, op. cit.

personally established nine, the last mission being that of San Buenaventura in 1782. Each mission was about 30 miles from the previous one or a day's walk. They were all linked by a dirt road which was called "El Camino Real." The purpose of each mission was to educate the Indios in the Catholic Faith and to teach them how to farm and build. Serra's unusual ability to accomplish these purposes in a peaceful way set him apart from all the other explorers.

(b) The Catholic community comprised a very small percentage of the colonial American population around the time of the American Revolution. The British formally abandoned any claims to the United States with the Treaty of Paris in 1783. Though many Catholics had fought on the Revolutionary side and some Catholics played a very prominent role, there was a distinct disdain toward them and they were considered second class citizens. There were also some instances of persecution. At the time, there were very few priests and religious and very few parishes. Two men who played a key role in helping establish the Catholic Church in America were John Carroll[7] and Blessed Junípero Serra.[8]

John Carroll was the first Roman Catholic bishop and archbishop in the United States. He was the younger brother of Daniel Carroll who was one of only five men to sign both the Articles of Confederation and the Constitution of the United States, and a cousin of Charles Carroll, the only Catholic signatory of the Declaration of Independence and the first American Senator from Maryland.

---

[7] See N.C. Eberhardt, *A Survey of American Church History*, St. Louis: B. Herder Book Co. (1964); J.G. Shea, *Life and Times of the Most Rev. John Carroll, Bishop and First Archbishop of Baltimore: Embracing the History of the Catholic Church in the United States 1763-1815*, Kessinger Publishing (2007); Hennesey, op. cit.

[8] See n. 60 (a).

Carroll joined the Society of Jesus in 1753. He studied in Europe, and after being ordained a priest in 1769, stayed there until the papal dissolution of the Society. Then he returned to Maryland where he became a missionary in that State and in Virginia. At the time, due to discrimination against Catholics, there was no public Catholic church in Maryland. He founded St. John the Evangelist Parish at Forest Glen in Maryland in 1774. The American Continental Congress, in 1776, asked Carroll, his cousin Charles Carroll, Samuel Chase, and Benjamin Franklin to travel to Quebec and attempt to convince the French Canadian population to join the revolution. The mission failed, but it made John Carroll well known to the infant United States government. Subsequently, in 1783, the Catholic Church was organized in Maryland. At the time the American Missions were still technically under the canonical jurisdiction of the Vicar Apostolic of the London District, Bishop James Talbot. Once appointed to this office in 1781, he refused to exercise jurisdiction over them. The Papal Nuncio to France, Archbishop Giuseppe Maria Doria Pamphilj, met Benjamin Franklin, the American ambassador in Paris, with the intent to resolve the impasse. Franklin advised the Papal Nuncio that the separation of Church and State in the United States prohibited the government to have any official opinion on such matters but privately suggested that perhaps a French bishop could be appointed to oversee the growing Roman Catholic community in the United States. The Holy See noted Franklin's high esteem of John Carroll. Consequently, Pius VI, in June 1784, appointed John Carroll as the provisional Superior of the American Missions. Carroll, in his new capacity and anticipating Vatican II by some two hundred years, promoted the reading of Scripture and the celebration of the Liturgy in the vernacular, instituted financial reform and lay involvement on the parish level, published articles in defense of the Catholic Church against the pronounced bigotry then rampant in the new nation, and encouraged cooperation between Catholics and Protestants in helping build the new nation.

The American clergy realized the need for a bishop, but did not want a foreign prelate. Therefore, having been assured by the Continental Congress that it would post no objections, they petitioned permission from the Holy See, in March 1788, to elect a bishop. Pius VI granted the permission the following July and in April 1789, they elected John Carroll as their first bishop. The election was approved by the Pope on 6th November 1789, appointing Carroll as the first Roman Catholic bishop in the United States. Carroll would be the only bishop elected by the clergy in the United States. He was ordained bishop in Dorset, England, in August 1790. He returned to the United States soon thereafter, taking up residence in Baltimore. He presided over the first Diocesan Synod the following year.

# CHAPTER NINETEEN

# Our Shining Stars: Holy Women and Men

When Europe was seeking Peace at Westphalia in 1648 so as to recover from the Thirty Years War, while Catholic monarchs tried to have complete control over the Church in their respective nations, when the Papacy was humiliated and Popes were prisoners, when Napoleon was waging his wars and remapping Europe, when heresies raged, when reactionary movements and secret societies appeared, the Catholic Church offered the world her saints.

## 61. Saintly People

Catholics should be proud of outstanding men and women who adhered to the Lord until the end. They came from all walks of life. They were members of nobility, peasants, widows, former soldiers, converts to Catholicism, scholars and slow-witted, emigrants, social and educational organizers and innovators, professionals in the medical and legal fields, religious women and men, missionaries, preachers, priests, bishops, and Popes. When the Catholic Church had to rise to confront corruption within, aggression from outside, and war among Christian nations, these humble men and women stood out as a challenge and a reminder that the Lord was still very much alive in His Church.[1] The following list is not exhaustive, but it might serve as an indication of the fidelity to the Lord and to His Church of people who came from all walks of life.

The year of peace among the European nations of 1648 was marked with the martyrdom in China of the Spanish Dominican priest Francisco Ferdinando de Capillas. He is the protomartyr of the official one hundred and thirty-four Chinese martyrs, mostly native lay persons. Tens of thousands were persecuted and martyred over the next two centuries and beyond. The year also marked the death of the Spaniard Peter Calasanz, the founder of the Piarists. He offered free education to the children of all classes of society in an age where one's social status did matter. On the other hand, the desperate plight of the sick that were poor in Genoa was counteracted by the noblewoman and peacemaker Virginia Centurione Bracelli who died in 1651. A similar undertaking, but this time to slaves, was that of the Spanish Jesuit Peter Claver who ministered tirelessly to slaves taken from Africa and shipped mercilessly to Colombia. He poured out his life in ministering to them, baptizing some 300,000, and fighting for their basic human rights. He died in 1654.

The Jesuits supplied the Church with many martyrs. Andrew Bobola was ministering to Catholics in Lithuania when he was captured, tortured, and martyred at the hands of the Cossacks of Chmielnicki in 1657. Jean de Brébeuf, Gabriel Lallerment, Noël Chabanel, Charles Garnier, Antoine Daniel were ministering

---

[1]   See D. Attwater, C.R. John, *The Penguin Dictionary of Saints*, 3rd edition, NY: Penguin Books (1993); O. Cary, *A History of Christianity in Japan*, Routledge: Curzon (1995); M. Bunson *et al*, *Our Sunday Visitor's Encyclopedia of Saints*, Huntington, IN: OSV (2003), see under different names of Saints and Blesseds; Kelly, op. cit.; *CE*, see under different names of Saints and Blesseds.

among the Hurons in Canada until they were martyred in 1649. They are numbered among the North American Martyrs.

The Dominican bishop Terence O'Brien of Emly, Ireland, was executed in Ireland in 1651 for resisting the systematic eradication of Catholicism in Ireland under Cromwell. He is one of the seventeen Irish martyrs. On the other hand, the first Irish saint to be canonized in about seven hundred years was Oliver Plunkett, Archbishop of Armagh and Primate of All Ireland. He was executed in 1681 for fulfilling his priestly duties toward his persecuted Irish flock. The English Jesuit Philip Evans and the Welsh secular priest John Lloyd ministered to their Welsh congregation for which reason they were executed in Cardiff in 1679, joining the Forty Martyrs of England and Wales, along with the Jesuits David Lewis and William Ireland, the secular priests John Kemble and John Plessington, the Benedictine Thomas Pickering who were martyred in England that same year. The secular priest Nicholas Postgate was executed in 1679 for being a Catholic priest.

The Frenchwoman Louise de Marillac[2] joined Vincent de Paul[3] in his ministry to the poor and the founding of the Daughters of Charity. She set up the oldest hospital in Paris, expanding the ministry of her Daughters to orphans, the elderly, the mentally disturbed, prisoners, and even maimed soldiers before her death in 1660.

There was the slow-witted Joseph of Cupertino who, like Didacus Joseph of Cadiz in the following century, put to shame the most brilliant minds by the depth of holiness the Lord so lavishly bestowed upon him. He was maltreated by some of his superiors, lived some years in exile, was silenced, and even brought

---

[2]  See Spiteri, III, 38 (e).
[3]  See ibid.

before the Inquisition in Naples where he was kept for several weeks until he was found innocent. He died in 1663.

The teen-age Filipino Blessed Pedro Calungsod went with the Spanish Jesuit Diego Luis de San Vitores to preach the Gospel in Guam where they were martyred in 1672. Four years later, they were joined in martyrdom by the Spanish priest Juan de los Reyes. Next, in 1685, the Filipino Jesuit lay-brother Phelippe Songsong died from wounds which he had received six months earlier.

The French priest John Eudes[4] was very concerned about the poor preparation of candidates to the priesthood. He, thus, established the Eudist Congregation for the education of priests and for missionary work. He preached all over France and invited people to live a moral life, promoting devotion to the Sacred Hearts of Jesus and Mary. He also established the Sisters of Our Lady of Charity of the Refuge, dedicated to abandoned women who were usually forced into prostitution. He died in 1680, the same year that Kateri Tekakwita, called the Lily of the Mohawks, died in Canada.

The last year of the seventeenth century witnessed the death of Marguerite Bourgeoys, foundress of the Congregation of Notre Dame. She was a very adventurous French woman who traveled from her homeland to Canada, where she founded a community of women dedicated to educating children without discrimination of their social status.

The Frenchman John Baptist de La Salle died in 1719, having spent much of his life dedicated to spiritually and academically educating poor children, reforming the French school system with lasting effects down to our own times. He pioneered programs that trained lay teachers and involved the parents of students. He

---

[4]   See, Spiteri, *At Your Fingertips* III, 38 (d).

founded the de La Salle Brothers, the first community of men in the Church which did not include priests. On the other hand, Jeanne Delanoue was the youngest of twelve children. She was originally involved in the family hotel business, always working to make more money. Undergoing a spiritual conversion, she gave up the family business and committed her life to the caring of the poor until her death in 1736. She founded the Congregation of St. Anne of Providence who serve the poor and needy.

Veronica Giulani, a Poor Clare nun, was an Italian mystic who died in 1727. She received the stigmata in 1697 and lived in constant pain for the rest of her life. Her incorrupt body lies in the Poor Clares convent at Città di Castello, Italy. Another Italian, Rosa Venerini, founded more than forty schools for the spiritual and social formation of girls and to train school teachers before dying in 1728. Clement XI, joined by eight Cardinals, attended one of her lessons and afterwards thanked her for the great service she was doing in Rome. One of her assistants in this endeavor was another Saint, Lucy Filipini who preceded her in death in 1732.

The nobleman Alphonsus Maria Liguori was born in Campagnia, Italy. He was a good musician, painter, and poet. He was also a prolific writer in moral theology and Mariology, founder of the Congregation of the Most Holy Redeemer (Redemptorists), and declared a Doctor of the Church for his incisive and profound contribution to Moral Theology. He went to law school in his mid-teens and became a well sought after lawyer. After losing an important case, he decided to abandon law and study for the priesthood. He was ordained a priest at age thirty and immediately embarked on ministering to the homeless and marginalized youth of Naples. He founded the "Evening Chapels," places for prayer, preaching, community, social activities and education, and ran by the youth themselves. By the time of his death, there were some ten thousand active members. Alphonsus founded the Redemptorists in 1732, a community whose purpose was to teach and preach in city slums and poor places. He also founded the female side of the Congregation with Sister Maria Celeste Crostarosa. Alphonsus and his followers preached against Jansenism. He was consecrated Bishop of Sant'Agatha dei Goti in 1762, against his will. During this time, his writings became very prolific. He was allowed to resign the office of Bishop in 1775, retired to the Redemptorist community at Pagani and died there in 1787, aged ninety. One of his early followers was the nobleman Januarius Maria Sarnell, who died in 1744. After his father had prohibited him from becoming a Jesuit, he studied law and became well known in the legal profession. He was also renowned for his devotion to the Blessed Sacrament and to visiting the incurably sick. He abandoned his lucrative legal profession and became a priest at age thirty. He joined St. Alphonsus three years later in the founding of the Redemptorists. He became famous for his moral writings and preaching. A fellow Redemptorist was Gerard Majella who grew up very poor after his father's death. After being turned down by the Capuchins, he became a Redemptorist. When a pregnant woman accused him of being the father of her child, he did not defend himself. Later she recanted and cleared him. Gerard was known to read the inmost thoughts in a person's heart. He died of tuberculosis at age twenty-nine in 1755.

It is estimated that between 130,000 and 300,000 Catholics have been martyred in Vietnam during the seventeenth, eighteenth and nineteenth centuries. Known Catholics at the time were branded on their faces for their Christian identity, while families and villages were annihilated because of their Christian faith. Their list is headed by the Vietnamese priest Andrew Dung-Lac, martyred in 1839. Since most of the names of these martyrs are lost to history, only one hundred and seventeen of them were formally canonized. Eleven Spanish Dominicans and ten French members of the Paris Foreign Missions Society are numbered among them.

The Italian noblewoman Anna Maria Redi joined the Cloistered Discalced Carmelite nuns in Florence, taking the name of Teresa Margarita of the Sacred Heart of Jesus. She lived a quiet life of contemplation until her death in 1770 at age twenty-three.

The French Canadian woman, Marie-Marguerite d'Youville founded the Sisters of Charity (the Grey Nuns) in Montreal for the purpose of looking after the poor. She had married Francois d'Youville, a bootlegger, and the couple had six children. She lost her father, her husband and four of her children when she was thirty. Her reaction to this great tragedy was to turn to God and to make His compassionate love known. She and three other companions founded a religious association to provide a home for the poor in Montreal in 1737. This move went against the grain of current society and she and her followers were scorned and called "grey women," which at the time meant "drunken women." But her followers grew in number and they became a religious community in 1744. She died in 1771.

The Savoyard mystic Paul of the Cross founded the Passionist congregation in 1720. He preached that the Passion of Jesus Christ is the most overwhelming sign of God's love for each individual and at the same time the door to union with our Redeemer. Originally, he and his brother John Baptist went around preaching and giving retreats at seminaries and religious houses. The community grew gradually. He also founded the contemplative Passionist Sisters. However, one of the persons who St. Paul had discouraged a number of times from joining the Passionists was Vincent Strambi. He is a great example of perseverance and courage. He was a bright, athletic, and troublesome child who straightened his life during his teen years. His life would prove to be very adventurous! While in the local seminary, he felt attracted to the religious life but was turned away by both the Capuchins and the Vincentians. He met St. Paul of the Cross while making a retreat at a Passionist monastery and asked the Saint to receive him into the community. Paul of the Cross, thinking that the young seminarian did not have the stamina for the austere Passionist lifestyle, refused the request. Vincent was ordained a priest but did not give up on the Passionists. Eventually Paul of the Cross acceded and the young priest joined the community. He soon became renowned for his preaching. Following the death of Paul of the Cross in 1775, Vincent was entrusted with several high offices in his community. After Napoleon invaded the Papal States and issued his anti-Catholic decrees, Vincent fled to Rome in 1798 and was a temporary prisoner of the French in 1799. Subsequently, he returned to Rome. When Pius VI died, Vincent was considered for the Papacy during the famous conclave in Venice. He was appointed Bishop of Macerata and Tolentino in July 1801, the first Passionist bishop. He soon became known for his great concern of the poor, the aged, the education of priests, and the formation of seminarians. He refused to provide a list of young men in his diocese suitable for French military service, refused to allow the reading in church of Napoleon's decree of the annexation of Macerate to the French Empire, and refused to take the oath of allegiance to France. He was first put under house arrest and then exiled in 1809. He was allowed to return to his diocese in 1814 and soon began the restoration of his devastated diocese and his people. He died in 1824.

The Frenchwoman Josephine Leroux, an Ursuline nun, was one of the many Catholics who were martyred during the

French Reign of Terror. She fled to Mons when monasteries and convents were suppressed during the Revolution but returned to Valenciennes in 1793. She was apprehended with several other nuns the following year and guillotined with ten other nuns for the crime of being Catholic. However, the last Catholic martyrs during the Reign of Terror were a group of sixteen Discalced Carmelite nuns from the monastery of Compiegne. They were guillotined on 17ᵗʰ July 1794.

Julie Billiart was the foundress of the Congregation of the Sisters of Notre Dame de Namur. She became partially paralyzed at age twenty-two and confined to her bed for the same number of years. She had suffered a shock when someone fired at her father. From her bed, she led a small group of high society ladies in the interior life. Over time, all of them abandoned Julie except for her friend, the Viscountess Francoise Blin de Bourdon who, like Julie, had survived the ravages of the French Revolution. These two, in 1803, laid the foundations for the Sisters of Notre Dame. Julie was cured of her paralysis in the middle of 1804. In the meantime they had been joined by two more women and their community became dedicated to the Christian education of girls and the training of religious teachers. By 1806, the community had grown to thirty and received the approval of Napoleon's government. Subsequently, members were sent all over France and Belgium. She died in 1816.

The United States was blessed with the life and apostolic ministry of Elizabeth Ann Bayley Seton, a convert to Catholicism, a mother, a young widow, a foundress, and the first native-born Saint of the United States. As a young Catholic widow she opened a school in New York, but the project soon failed due to the anti-Catholic bigotry. She then met Louis Dubourg, a French Sulpician priest who was a refugee from the Reign of Terror. The

Sulpicians at the time were in the process of establishing the first seminary in the States.[5] After some trying and difficult years, Elizabeth Ann accepted Dubourg's invitation to open a school and moved to Emmitsburg, Maryland, in 1809. She opened St. Joseph's Academy the following year. Eventually, Elizabeth Ann was able to establish the first religious non-cloistered community in the United States, called Sisters of Charity of St. Joseph. Their school was the first free Catholic school in the States. She died in 1821.

Finally, while the year of revolutions, 1848, was ravaging continental Europe, a small Italian Passionist priest who emigrated to England, Dominic Barberi, was coming to the closing of his ministry. His parents had died when he was a small boy and he was adopted by his maternal uncle, growing up on a farm. He could not enter the religious life because such communities had been suppressed in French-occupied Italian territories. After they were re-established in the Papal States in 1814, Dominic joined the Passionists. Soon after his ordination as priest in 1818, he became convinced that God wanted him to minister in Protestant England. But this was to take place many years later and after many personal sufferings. In the meantime he taught philosophy and theology to fellow Passionists and published. The call to go to England came in 1830 through some prominent English Catholics. But he was kept in Italy, fulfilling some responsible appointments in his community. The Passionist leadership agreed to make a foundation in Ere, Belgium, in 1840 and assigned Dominic as the superior of the Belgian mission. After some initial very serious problems, the community began to take root. Later

---

[5]  The seminary was Mount St. Mary's College and Seminary which is still flourishing today.

that year, Dominic was invited by Bishop Nicholas Wiseman[6] to make a foundation at Aston Hall in England. Dominic made his final journey to England in 1841 and his ministry inaugurated the second spring of Catholicism in Britain, despite the fact that initially even Catholics held him in suspicion and in the fear that a new persecution of Catholics would begin. In time, Dominic began to receive a string of converts, one of whom was the famous John Henry Newman, the first person to be beatified as an English non-martyr since before the English Reformation. Dominic died in 1849, while Cardinal Newman died in 1890. Like stars across the skies, these holy men and women, our brothers and sisters, shine across the orb of history.

---

[6] Bishop Wiseman became the first Archbishop of Westminster upon the re-establishment of the Catholic hierarchy in England and Wales in 1850. He was created Cardinal that same year.